GCSE 9–1
LORD
OF THE FLIES

BY WILLIAM GOLDING

SCHOLASTIC

Author Cindy Torn

Reviewer Rob Pollard

Editorial team Rachel Morgan, Audrey Stokes, Lesley Densham, Kate Pedlar

Typesetting Jayne Rawlings/Oxford Raw Design

Cover design Dipa Mistry and Jason Cox

App development Hannah Barnett, Phil Crothers and RAIOSOFT International Pvt Ltd

Acknowledgements

Illustration Rupert Van Wyk @ Beehive Illustration

Photographs
pages 12 and 82: conch shell, Eivaisla/Shutterstock; pages 15 and 81: glasses, Miyuki Satake/Shutterstock; page 17: fire, Krumao/Shutterstock; pages 23, 54 and 63: spear, Juan Aunion/Shutterstock; page 25: broken glasses, Miiisha/Shutterstock; pages 28 and 74: honeybee, Peter Waters/Shutterstock; page 30: blue flower, Krivosheev Vitaly/Shutterstock; page 32: knife, sema srinouljan/Shutterstock; wild boar, Michalicenko/Shutterstock; page 34: jungle, iordani/Shutterstock; page 35: wild boar and piglets, WildMedia/Shutterstock; page 38: snake, Narupon Nimpaiboon/Shutterstock; page 41: lightning, PhotoVisions/Shutterstock; page 50: red granite, vilax/Shutterstock; page 65: gilt buttons, Five Object Shop/Shutterstock; pages 59 and 69: lightning, Triff/Shutterstock; pages 72 and 80: blood splatters, Mrspopman1985/Shutterstock; page 73: nuclear bomb explosion, Romolo Tavani/Shutterstock; page 78: palm tree, DNY59/iStock; Garden of Eden, Basheera Designs/Shutterstock; page 82: wooden cross, Lunatictm/Shutterstock; page 90: girl sitting exam, Monkey Business Images/Shutterstock; page 93: notepad and pen, TRINACRIA PHOTO/Shutterstock

Published in the UK by Scholastic Education, 2019
Scholastic Education, Scholastic Distribution Centre, Bosworth Avenue, Tournament Fields, Warwick, CV34 6UQ
Scholastic Ireland, 89E Lagan Road, Dublin Industrial Estate, Glasnevin, Dublin, D11 HP5F

SCHOLASTIC and associated logos are trademarks and/or registered trademarks of Scholastic Inc.

www.scholastic.co.uk

© 2019 Scholastic

2 3 4 5 6 7 8 9 3 4 5 6 7 8 9 0 1 2

A CIP catalogue record for this book is available from the British Library.
ISBN 978-1407-18326-8

This book is made of materials from well-managed, FSC®-certified forests and other controlled sources.

Designed using Adobe InDesign

Note from the publisher:
Please use this product in conjunction with the official specification and sample assessment materials. Ask your teacher if you are unsure where to find them.

Contents

How to use this book 4

Features of this guide 6

An introduction to your AQA modern text 8

Character tree of *Lord of the Flies* 9

Timeline of *Lord of the Flies* 10

Chronological section   **12**

    Chapters One, Two, Three and Four 12

    Chapters Five, Six, Seven and Eight 26

    Chapters Nine, Ten, Eleven and Twelve 40

Characters   **56**

    Ralph 56

    Jack 58

    Simon 60

    Piggy 61

    Sam and Eric 62

    Roger 63

    Littluns 64

    Review it 65

Themes and contexts   **66**

    Savagery versus civilisation 66

    End of innocence 68

    Power 69

    Politics 70

    Context 72

    Review it 75

Language, structure and form   **76**

    Language 76

    Structure 79

    Form 81

    Review it 83

Doing well in your AQA exam   **84**

    Understanding the question 84

    Planning your answer 85

    What your AQA examiner is looking for 86

    Writing your answer 88

    Going for the top grades 90

    Review it 91

AQA exam-style questions   **92**

Glossary   **94**

Check your answers on the free revision app or at www.scholastic.co.uk/gcse

How to use this book

This Study Guide is designed to help you prepare effectively for your AQA GCSE English literature exam question on *Lord of the Flies* (Paper 2, Section A).

The content has been organised in a sequence that builds confidence, and which will deepen your knowledge and understanding of the novel step by step. Therefore, it is best to work through this book in the order that it is presented.

This Study Guide uses the Faber and Faber edition.

HOW TO REVISE!

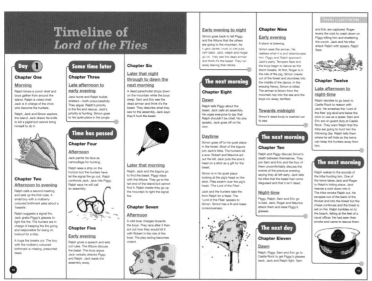

Know the plot

1

It is very important that you know the plot well: to be clear about what happens and in what order. The **timeline** on pages 10–11 provides a useful overview of the plot, highlighting key events.

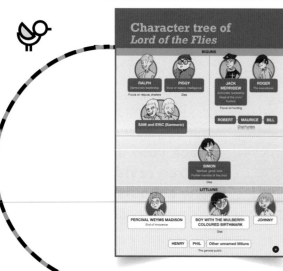

The **character tree** on page 9 introduces you to the main characters of the text.

The chronological section

2

The chronological section on pages 12–55 takes you through the novel, chapter by chapter, providing plot summaries and pointing out important details. It is also designed to help you think about the structure of the novel.

This section provides an in-depth exploration of themes or character development, drawing your attention to how Golding's language choices reveal the novel's meaning.

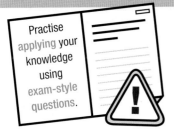

Practise applying your knowledge using exam-style questions.

The novel as a whole

3

The second half of the guide is retrospective: it helps you to look back over the whole novel through a number of relevant 'lenses': characters, themes, Golding's language, form and structural features.

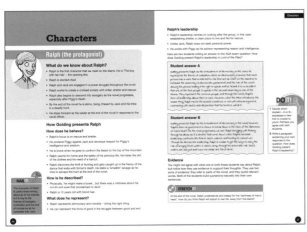

Doing well in your AQA Exam

Stick to the **TIME LIMITS** you will need to in the exam.

4

Finally, you will find an extended 'Doing well in your AQA exam' section which guides you through the process of understanding questions, and planning and writing answers.

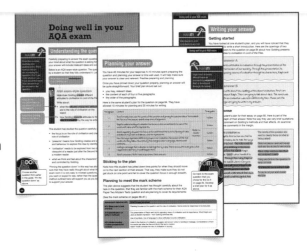

Features of this guide

The best way to retain information is to take an active approach to revision.

Throughout this book, you will find lots of features that will make your revision an active, successful process.

SNAPIT!

Use the Snap it! feature in the revision app to take pictures of key concepts and information. Great for revision on the go!

DEFINEIT!

Explains the meaning of difficult words from the set texts.

Callouts Additional explanations of important points.

Words shown in **purple bold** can be found in the glossary on page 94.

Find methods of relaxation that work for you throughout the revision period.

Regular exercise helps stimulate the brain and will help you relax.

DOIT!

Activities to embed your knowledge and understanding and prepare you for the exams.

NAILIT!

Succinct and vital tips on how to do well in your exam.

STRETCHIT!

Provides content that stretches you further.

REVIEW IT!

Helps you to consolidate and understand what you have learned before moving on.

Revise in pairs or small groups and deliver presentations on topics to each other.

FOR HIGH-MARK QUESTIONS, SPEND TIME **PLANNING** YOUR ANSWER!

AQA exam-style question

AQA exam-style sample questions based on the extract shown are given on some pages. Use the sample mark scheme on page 86 to help you assess your responses. This will also help you understand what you could do to improve your response.

FREE REVISION APP

- The **free revision app** can be downloaded to your mobile phone (iOS and Android), making **on-the-go revision** easy.

- Use the revision calendar to help map out your revision in the lead-up to the exam.

- Complete multiple-choice questions and create your own SNAP**IT!** revision cards.

www.scholastic.co.uk/gcse

Online answers and additional resources
All of the tasks in this book are designed to get you thinking and to consolidate your understanding through thought and application. Therefore, it is important to write your own answers before checking. Some questions include tables where you need to fill in your answer in the book. Other questions require you to use a separate piece of paper so that you can draft your response and work out the best way of answering.

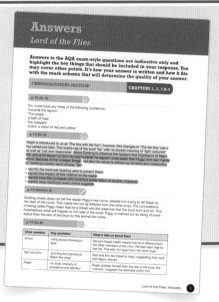

Get plenty of sleep, especially the night before an exam.

LOOK AFTER YOURSELF

Help your brain by looking after your whole body!

Once you have worked through a section, you can check your answers to Do it!, Stretch it!, Review it! and the exam practice sections on the app or at **www.scholastic.co.uk/gcse**.

Why study *Lord of the Flies*?

Although *Lord of the Flies* was written more than 60 years ago, it has kept its appeal for modern audiences. The subject matter of the novel still has a strong immediate relevance. We are presented with a scene from an adventure story with a group of boys stranded on an isolated island following a plane crash. With their survival at stake, the boys begin to set up their own version of civilisation.

How many modern teenagers have concerns about what is civilised and what is right? How many teenagers today wonder what would happen if the rules disappeared from our society? How many teenagers worry what will happen if the bullies win? The plot of *Lord of the Flies* gives powerful expression to all these familiar feelings and experiences.

Lord of the Flies in your AQA exam

Lord of the Flies is examined in Section A (the first part) of the second AQA GCSE English Literature exam, Paper 2 Modern texts and poetry. Here is how it fits into the overall assessment framework:

Paper 1 Time: **1 hour 45 minutes**	Paper 2 Time: **2 hours 15 minutes**
Section A: Shakespeare	**Section A: Modern prose or drama:** *Lord of the Flies*
Section B: 19th-century novel	Section B: Poetry anthology
	Section C: Unseen poetry

There will be **two** questions on *Lord of the Flies*. You must answer **one** of them and you should not answer questions on any other modern text (that is, any other novel or play). You should spend **45 minutes** planning and writing your answer to the question. There are 30 marks available for the *Lord of the Flies* question, plus four extra marks for good **vocabulary, spelling, sentences and punctuation** (VSSP, sometimes called 'SPaG').

Your *Lord of the Flies* question will focus on character and/or theme. You must answer the question in relation to the extract and to relevant other parts of the play that you have chosen for yourself.

A character tree

The 'character tree' on page 9 should help you to fix in your mind the names of the characters, their relationships and who did what to whom.

Timeline of *Lord of the Flies*

The timeline on pages 10–11 provides a visual overview of the plot, highlighting key events which take place over the course of the novel. It will also help you to think about the structure of the novel.

Character tree of *Lord of the Flies*

BIGUNS

RALPH
Democratic leadership

Focus on rescue, shelters

PIGGY
Voice of reason, intelligence

Dies

JACK MERRIDEW
Autocratic leadership
Head of the choir/hunters

Focus on hunting

ROGER
The executioner

SAM and ERIC (Samneric)
Followers

ROBERT — **MAURICE** — **BILL**

Choir/hunters

SIMON
Spiritual, good, kind
Former member of the choir

Dies

LITTLUNS

PERCIVAL WEYMS MADISON
End of innocence

BOY WITH THE MULBERRY-COLOURED BIRTHMARK

Dies

JOHNNY

HENRY — **PHIL** — **Other unnamed littluns**

The general public

Timeline of *Lord of the Flies*

Day 1

Chapter One

Morning

Ralph blows a conch shell and boys gather from around the island. Ralph is voted chief. Jack is in charge of the choir, who become the hunters.

Ralph, Jack and Simon explore the island. Jack draws his knife to kill a piglet but cannot bring himself to do it.

Chapter Two
Afternoon to evening

Ralph calls a second meeting and sets up the first rules. A small boy with a mulberry-coloured birthmark asks about a 'beastie'.

Ralph suggests a signal fire. Jack grabs Piggy's glasses to light the fire. The hunters are in charge of keeping the fire going and responsible for being on lookout for a ship.

A huge fire breaks out. The boy with the mulberry-coloured birthmark is missing, presumed dead.

Some time later

Chapter Three

Late afternoon to early evening

Jack hunts and Ralph builds shelters – both unsuccessfully. They argue. Ralph's priority is the fire and rescue. Jack's priority is hunting. Simon goes to his quiet place in the jungle.

Time has passed

Chapter Four

Afternoon

Jack paints his face as camouflage for hunting.

Ralph sees a ship on the horizon but the hunters have let the signal fire go out. Ralph confronts Jack. Jack hits Piggy. Ralph says he will call an assembly.

Chapter Five

Early evening

Ralph gives a speech and sets out rules. The littluns discuss the beast. The boys argue. Jack verbally attacks Piggy and Ralph. Jack leads the assembly away.

Chapter Six

Later that night through to dawn the next morning

A dead parachutist drops down on the mountain while the boys sleep. Sam and Eric see the dead airman and think it's the beast. They describe what they saw to the assembly. Jack says they'll hunt the beast.

Later that morning

Ralph, Jack and the biguns go to find the beast. Piggy stays with the littluns. They go to the tail-end of the island but cannot find it. Ralph insists they go up the mountain to light the signal fire.

Chapter Seven

Afternoon

A wild boar charges towards the boys. They race after it then act out how they would kill it with Robert in the role of the boar. The play-acting becomes violent.

Early evening to night

Simon goes back to tell Piggy and the littluns that the others are going to the mountain. As it gets darker, most of the boys turn back. Jack, Ralph and Roger go on. They see the dead airman and think it's the beast. They run away leaving their sticks.

The next morning

Chapter Eight

Dawn

Ralph tells Piggy about the beast. Jack calls an assembly. He urges everyone to say that Ralph shouldn't be chief. No one speaks. Jack goes off on his own.

Daytime

Simon goes off to his quiet place in the forest. Most of the biguns join Jack's tribe. The hunters kill a sow. Robert and Maurice act out the kill. Jack puts the sow's head on a stick as a gift for the beast.

Simon is in his quiet place looking at the pig's head on the stick. Flies swarm over the pig's head, 'The Lord of the Flies'.

Jack and the hunters take fire from Ralph for a feast. The 'Lord of the Flies' speaks to Simon. Simon has a fit and loses consciousness.

Chapter Nine

Early evening

A storm is brewing.

Simon sees the airman. He realises what it is and disentangles him. Piggy and Ralph approach Jack's party. Tempers flare and the boys begin to dance as the storm breaks. At first, Roger is in the role of the pig. Simon crawls out of the forest and stumbles into the middle of the dance. In the ensuing frenzy, Simon is killed. The airman is blown from the mountain top into the sea and the boys run away, terrified.

Towards midnight

Simon's dead body is washed out to sea.

The next morning

Chapter Ten

Ralph and Piggy discuss Simon's death between themselves. They join Sam and Eric and the four of them uncomfortably discuss the events of the previous evening, saying they all left early. Jack tells his tribe that the beast had come disguised and that it isn't dead.

Night-time

Piggy, Ralph, Sam and Eric go to bed. Jack, Roger and Maurice attack them and steal Piggy's glasses.

The next day

Chapter Eleven

Dawn

Ralph, Piggy, Sam and Eric go to Castle Rock to get Piggy's glasses back. Jack and Ralph fight. Sam

and Eric are captured. Roger levers the rock to crash down on Piggy killing him and shattering the conch. Jack and his tribe attack Ralph with spears. Ralph flees.

Chapter Twelve

Late afternoon to night-time

Ralph decides to go back to Castle Rock to reason with Jack. He smashes the 'Lord of the flies' pig skull and takes the stick to use as a spear. Sam and Eric are on guard duty at Castle Rock. They warn Ralph that the tribe are going to hunt him the following day. Ralph tells them where he will hide so the twins can keep the hunters away from him.

The next morning

Ralph wakes to the sounds of the tribe hunting him. One of the twins takes Jack and Roger to Ralph's hiding place. Jack heaves a rock down into it. The tribe smoke Ralph out. He escapes out of the back of the thicket and into the forest but the chase continues and the forest is set on fire. Ralph tumbles on to the beach, falling at the feet of a naval officer. He had seen their smoke and came to rescue them.

Chapter One: The Sound of the Shell

Summary

We are introduced to 'The boy with fair hair' in an exotic jungle **setting** as he heads towards a lagoon. Wearing school uniform, he is soon joined by another boy wearing 'a greasy wind-breaker' who is 'very fat'. The boys realise that they are on an island, they have survived a plane crash and most importantly there are no adults. The fair boy is Ralph. The fat boy – whose name we never know – confides that he was called 'Piggy' at school and asks Ralph not to tell anyone. Piggy tells Ralph about the 'atom bomb', knowing there would be few survivors in the outside world. Ralph is sure that his father will 'come and rescue' them. They find a conch. Piggy explains how to make a sound with it. Ralph tries, and finally, the resulting sound draws out other boys. The boys look to Ralph for direction as Piggy begins to take names.

A 'dark' shape moves along the beach towards the group – the choir and Jack Merridew arrive. Ralph betrays Piggy by telling the new arrivals Piggy's nickname, and suggests that the group should have a chief. Although Jack assumes that he should be chief, when the boys vote they decide that it should be Ralph. Jack is offered control of the choir, who will be 'hunters'. Ralph and Jack, accompanied by Simon, go to explore and find out if it is an island. Piggy, humiliated, is left with the smaller boys to 'take names'.

Ralph, Jack and Simon explore and push a rock 'as large as a small motor car' off a cliff. After climbing to the top of a mountain, they realise they are on an island and that they are alone. As they head back, they find a small pig that has been caught in the creepers. Jack goes to kill it but pauses. The reader is told, 'Next time there would be no mercy.'

DEFINE IT!

asthma – a condition that causes difficulty in breathing

atom bomb – a nuclear bomb

conch – a large seashell

mirages – an optical illusion caused by atmospheric conditions

mortification – embarrassment and shame

DO IT!

In the opening paragraph, Golding quickly establishes that we are in an exotic setting. Find three **quotations** that help the reader to imagine this setting.

Introducing Ralph and Piggy: 'The fair boy' and 'the fat boy'

Ralph is the first **character** we meet on the island and he is the character throughout the novel that the reader gets to understand in the most detail. One of the first facts that we are given is about Ralph's hair. Look at this student's response when writing about Golding's presentation of Ralph in this scene:

> Ralph is introduced to us as 'The boy with fair hair'; however, this changes to 'The fair boy' just a few sentences later. This subtle use of the word 'fair' with its double meaning of 'light coloured' as well as 'just and reasonable' allows Golding to influence the reader's first impression of Ralph. Not only is he shown to 'pick his way towards the lagoon' more easily than Piggy, who can 'hardly move' because of the 'creeper things', but also his nature is defined as sensible and trustworthy by Golding's careful word choice, 'fair'.

Piggy is presented in this scene as out of place within the natural world. He can only see because of his 'specs', and his 'Ass-mar' means that any effort leaves him 'breathing hard'. His colloquial speech, 'All them other kids', and 'grubby wind-breaker' place him firmly as coming from a poorer background than Ralph and the other boys. The indignity of the effect of eating 'Them fruit' again reinforces Piggy's low status and Golding further establishes his place as the outsider when Ralph fails to ask his name in response to his 'proffer of acquaintance'.

Golding uses Piggy to supply the reader with details about the crash. Piggy knows that the plane was attacked, that the tube from the plane made the scar, and he quickly reasons that 'there's a lot more of us scattered about'. Most importantly, it is Piggy who knows how to blow the conch that gathers the other boys, and it is Piggy who suggests there should be a meeting and 'a list' of names.

NAIL IT!

Your AQA exam focuses on 'writers' methods' – this means anything that the writer does on purpose to make meaning.

DO IT!

In the student's answer (left), highlight where they:

- identify the methods Golding uses to present Ralph

- explain the impact of this method on the reader

- identify how this contrasts with Golding's presentation of another character

- explain what Golding's word choice suggests.

STRETCH IT!

Why do you think Golding does not tell the reader Piggy's real name? What are the **connotations** of 'Piggy' as a name?

13

Introducing Jack and the choir: 'something dark was fumbling along'

Described as a 'creature', Jack and the choir appear at the sound of the conch. Golding uses clothing throughout the novel to show the characteristics of the boys. The choir's clothing is 'strangely eccentric' as the boys moved in formation. The 'boy who controlled them' is described, vaulting on to the platform, as assured and confident 'with his cloak flying'.

Golding presents the physical contrasts between Ralph and Jack to highlight their different natures. Ralph with his 'fair hair' and 'golden body' has a 'mildness about his mouth' and eyes that 'proclaimed no devil'. Jack, however, has 'red hair' and is 'ugly without silliness'. His eyes, 'frustrated', are 'turning or ready to turn to anger'. Golding describes how Jack's 'simple arrogance' that he 'ought to be chief' is reduced to a 'blush of mortification' when Ralph is voted chief.

DOIT!

Golding introduces us to key characters. Find a key quotation from Chapter One for each of the characters below and explain what it tells us. Some have been completed to help you.

Character	Key quotation	What it tells us about them
Simon	'He's always throwing a faint'	
Sam and Eric		
Roger	'an inner intensity of avoidance and secrecy'	

NAILIT!

You will not have the text with you in your exam, so having a precise knowledge of pivotal parts of the novel will be essential.

STRETCHIT!

Golding shows a series of instances where Jack uses his knife in this chapter. What are they? What is Golding signalling to the reader?

Introducing violence: 'three of us will go on an expedition'

This expedition is important: during it we see the first intentional act of destruction by the boys as Ralph, Jack and Simon heave a boulder 'as large as a small motor car' over a cliff. This act 'shook' the forest 'as with the passage of an enraged monster'. Golding's **language** choices reflect the violence of the scene as the great rock 'smashed a deep hole in the canopy of the forest'.

As they explore further, Simon discovers the 'candle bushes.' This religious image is shattered by Jack's violent response as he 'slashed at one with his knife'. Soon after, the boys encounter a piglet caught in the creepers. Jack pauses and the piglet runs away; he excuses this pause by saying, 'I was just waiting for a moment to decide where to stab him.' Golding highlights how at this point the 'enormity' of 'cutting into living flesh' is too 'unbearable'.

Chapter Two: Fire on the Mountain

Summary

Ralph blows the conch to bring the boys to an assembly on the platform. He tells them that they are on an uninhabited island and Jack interrupts to tell the boys about the pigs. Jack lies when he says that the pig broke away before he could kill it. Ralph establishes the rule that holding the conch gives the person the right to speak. Ralph says it is a good island, containing everything they need until the adults rescue them. A small boy with a 'mulberry-coloured birthmark' asks what Ralph is going to do about the 'snake thing', the 'beastie'. Ralph tries to dismiss the story of the 'beastie' that 'came in the dark' with reason, but it is Jack, who says he will 'kill it', that calms their fears.

Ralph suggests building a fire on top of the mountain to make smoke to signal to a ship. The boys, delighted and distracted by this idea, rush off following Jack, leaving Ralph and Piggy. To Piggy's disgust, Ralph joins the boys and he works successfully with Jack in the 'strange invisible light of friendship'. It is only when they have built the pile of wood and leaves that they realise that they don't know how to light a fire. Suggestions are made, but when Piggy arrives, Jack uses Piggy's glasses as 'burning glasses', violently taking them from Piggy. The fire is lit and the race to feed it begins. Piggy realises that 'There wasn't any smoke. Only flame', and an argument takes place between Jack and Piggy with Jack saying that 'The conch doesn't count on top of the mountain' before saying that the choir will take responsibility for the fire. As the conflict between Jack and Piggy continues, the fire rages out of control, sweeping the island. The boys realise that the boy with the mulberry-coloured birthmark is not there.

DEFINE IT!

dubiety – doubt

fetch and miss – a breathing problem linked to asthma where the person takes a short gasp of breath before delaying the exhale

perpendicular – vertical, upright

recrimination – blame

DO IT!

Golding uses schoolboy **slang** 'Whee-oh!', 'Waaco!', 'Bong!', 'Doink!'.

How does this affect the way the reader views the boys?

Context: 'It's like in a book'

As Ralph is telling the boys that it is a 'good island', he says that 'It's like a book.' At this point, the boys begin listing books featuring islands. One of these books is *The Coral Island*. This book, written by RM Ballantyne, was published in 1858. In Ballantyne's novel, three boys shipwrecked on an island embark on looking after themselves before engaging in conflicts with cannibals and converting the natives to Christianity. The novel was very popular; however, Golding felt that boys would not behave as Ballantyne's characters did. He felt that unlike Ballantyne's characters, who retained all the rules of a civilised society, people left without any of society's restraints would descend into savagery. Golding wrote *Lord of the Flies* as an answer to this original novel – even using two of the character names – Jack and Ralph.

Look at this opening of an answer from a student writing about Golding's presentation of the island.

> Golding presents the island as a 'good island'. There is food, water and materials for shelter, everything the boys could need. It's presented as a paradise almost like the Garden of Eden. However, just like in Eden, there is a serpent - a force of evil. The boy with the birthmark asks about the 'beastie, the snake-thing'.

Add to this opening, showing Golding's presentation of the contrast between Ralph and Jack's reaction to the news of the 'snake-thing' by the boy with the mulberry-coloured birthmark.

STRETCH IT!

What does Golding present as the real evil in the island paradise?

Civilisation and society: 'We'll have rules!'

Within any society there has to be rules to provide order. Ralph creates the rule where holding the conch gives the person holding it the right to speak. Notice how Golding presents Piggy's respect for the conch, with 'one hand on the great shell' as he **interprets** for the boy with the mulberry-coloured birthmark.

Jack's response to the rules is different. He agrees with wanting 'lots of rules!' but his focus remains on the punishments that would be given out 'when anyone breaks 'em'. With the rule of the conch established, Jack very quickly sets out to undermine it, wanting to silence Piggy, the voice of reason, by saying 'The conch doesn't count on the top of the mountain.'

AQA exam-style question

How does Golding present Piggy?

Write about:

- what Piggy says and how he behaves
- how Golding uses Piggy to explore society and human nature.

[30 marks]

How Golding presents the fire on the mountain: 'You got your small fire all right.'

The island is presented as a paradise: 'this is a good island'. Ralph describes it as 'wizard' but Golding shows how quickly the boys' actions cause the destruction of this environment. In Chapter One, Ralph, Jack and Simon send a boulder smashing from a cliff into the canopy. In Chapter Two, the boys' lack of foresight causes a fire that results in similar effects to an atom bomb, as tree trunks 'crumbled to white dust'. It is ironic that the boys were being evacuated because of an atom bomb at home. Look carefully at how Golding builds the description of the fire step by step as the fire rampages out of control. He uses a subtle mix of positive language to describe the draw and the beauty of the fire –'yellow flames that poured upwards and shook a great beard of flame' – and negative language to reveal the devastating consequences of releasing this 'hell'.

'Stirred' suggests that the flames are waking up, gently. Notice that the flames are 'small'. This links to later images.

Crawling suggests animal-like movement. Its pace would be creeping or even sneaking.

> Small flames stirred at the bole of a tree and crawled away through leaves and brushwood, dividing and increasing. One patch touched a tree trunk and scrambled up like a bright squirrel.

Continuous action is suggested by the use of these verbs – this momentum is happening now and will continue to happen into the future.

'Scrambled' suggests a rapid but clumsy movement.

Simile used to describe the movement of the fire through the trees. It's a positive image; 'bright' suggests the light from the flames.

Carefully read the description of the fire in Chapter Two.

1 Find a further example of Golding's presentation of the fire using animal **imagery**.

2 What are the boys doing as the fire rages?

Chapter Three: Huts on the Beach

Summary

The chapter opens with Jack hunting. Time has passed and Jack is 'dog-like' in his concentration and intent. He is carrying a sharpened stick and, except for a pair of shorts, he is naked. Frustrated, he follows a trail of pig droppings before encountering a pig. Jack throws his spear but he is unsuccessful as the pig gets away.

Jack encounters Ralph and Simon building shelters on the beach. Ralph complains that the boys will only help for a while and then they disappear to play or go hunting. Like Jack, Ralph is also unsuccessful as two shelters are 'shaky' and one is a 'ruin'. Jack and Ralph clash as Jack tries to explain his compulsion to hunt but Ralph refuses to engage. Ralph moves to a 'safe subject', the boys' fear at night. It is ironic, of course, that fear should be a subject to move the conversation on to safer ground. Jack admits that he feels 'hunted' in the jungle. Simon says that it is almost as if 'the beastie or the snake-thing, was real'. This unsettles both Ralph and Jack as 'Snakes were not mentioned now.' The word has become taboo. Ralph still wants to focus on the fire. With separate obsessions: shelter and rescue versus hunting, Jack and Ralph cannot communicate.

Simon has wandered into the jungle. He shows his kind nature as he helps the littluns with fruit out of their reach. He enters a space in the jungle 'walled with dark aromatic bushes'. He sits there as evening begins to fall and the scent of the 'candle-like buds' spills out into the air and takes 'possession of the island'.

DEFINE IT!

unheeding – ignoring

node – lump

susurration – whispering or rustling

vicissitudes – variations

DO IT!

As Jack is hunting at the start of the chapter, what changes in him does Golding present to show that:

1 time has passed?

2 Jack is becoming more savage and uncivilised?

NAIL IT!

Your AQA exam question stem is always 'how [Golding] presents…'

- 'how' is about the methods Golding uses

- 'presents' is not just about what he is saying, but also his attitude towards that topic, and how he wants us to respond to it.

Conflict between Ralph and Jack: 'the antagonism was audible'

In this chapter, the differences between Ralph and Jack once more bubble to the surface. Ralph complains that the boys are more interested in the more instant pleasures of 'playing' or 'bathing' than building shelters for their security. Jack's mind is focused on hunting and killing.

Look how Golding structures the conversation between Ralph and Jack (from 'He tried to convey the compulsion to track down and kill...' to 'baffled in love and hate'). We can see the key elements of the conflict, their inability to see the other's point of view and how each of the boys tries to take control and steer the argument:

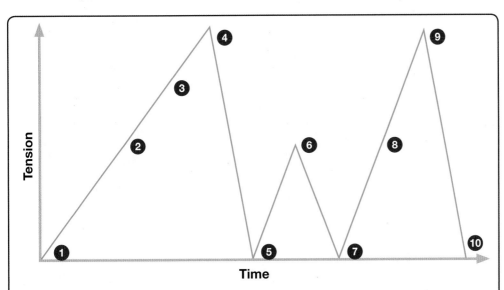

1 Jack tries to explain his 'compulsion to track down and kill'.

2 An exchange begins about hunting between Jack and Ralph. It's spoken in short, terse statements:
'but you didn't'
'I thought I might'
'But you haven't yet.'

3 Ralph asks Jack to help with the shelters, casually but 'with an undertone'.

4 Jack 'shouted in rage' and both boys end up 'red in the face'.

5 Ralph changes the subject and they discuss the littluns' fear of the 'beastie'.

6 Simon names the now taboo 'snake-thing'; both Ralph and Jack 'flinched' at the name.

7 Ralph and Jack reminisce about the expedition to bring back happier times, 'remembering the glamour of the first day'.

8 Jack tries to explain his fear, but Ralph is 'indignant'. Jack continues to obsess about hunting: Ralph obsesses about fire.

9 Ralph loses control, shouting, 'But you like it! You want to hunt! While I –'

10 They discuss Simon, agreeing, 'He's funny.'

They end up looking at each other 'baffled in love and hate'.

 STRETCHIT!

Golding describes Ralph and Jack as 'two continents of experience and feeling, unable to communicate'. What does he mean by this?

 **DO**IT!

Use different colours to highlight which of the following emotions apply to **Ralph**, **Jack** or **both** of the boys in this chapter.

**frustrated
intense
absorbed
brooding
irritated
compulsive
passionate
volatile
nostalgic
bewildered
exasperated**

Savagery: 'a furtive thing, ape-like among the tangle of trees'

Golding presents civilisation and savagery as opposites, with civilisation being fragile, shakily held together by rules. Ralph represents civilisation. His focus on shelter to provide security is the stability that civilisation offers. Jack represents savagery. At the start of this chapter, Golding presents Jack as 'dog-like' and 'ape-like', moving almost on all fours as he tracks the pigs. He is 'naked', his clothes – a symbol of the trappings of civilisation – are now reduced to just 'a pair of tattered shorts held up by his knife-belt'. Golding tells us that Jack's 'compulsion to track and kill' was 'swallowing him up', with this **metaphor** revealing his loss of humanity and civilisation. This is reiterated further when Jack 'had to think for a moment before he could remember what rescue was' as if even his language is escaping him as he descends into savagery.

Simon: 'He helps'

While this conflict is happening, Piggy is 'lying flat' looking into the water – just like the pigs Jack is going to hunt, and Simon takes himself quietly away. Simon does not engage in the power struggle despite being part of the conversation in its early stages. He also shows no fear of the 'beast'. Instead, he goes to be on his own and as he passes, he kindly and unselfishly helps the littluns by reaching the high, 'choicest' fruit in the same way that he tried to help Ralph with the shelters. As he moves through the creepers in the dense part of the jungle they 'shivered throughout their lengths', in contrast to how they ensnared Piggy in the opening chapter. The creepers have been shown to be like 'snakes', yet they have no hold on Simon. In fact, Golding's presentation of them shivering could suggest fear of him. Simon can be seen to represent humankind's goodness. Simon is shown in harmony with the island in this church-like space. This space is filled with the 'candle-buds' that take possession of the island at the end of the chapter.

DO IT!

Jack suggests that the hunters could 'paint their faces'. Explain why this is another step towards savagery.

Chapter Four: Painted Faces and Long Hair

Summary

Time continues to pass and the boys begin to accept the 'rhythm' of this new life. The morning is full of 'pleasures' and 'hope'. However, 'Strange things happened at midday' when the sea 'moved apart' – an effect that Piggy 'discounts' as a 'mirage' – before the boys are 'menaced' by 'untold terrors' as darkness falls.

Golding shows us the lives of the littluns, the six year olds. We see the misery of Percival, who 'played little and cried often' and the 'stomach-aches' and 'diarrhoea' caused by the boys' diet of fruit. Roger and Maurice cruelly destroy the littluns' decorated sandcastles but remain restricted by their memories of rules and civilisation. Maurice retains some of the 'unease of wrong-doing' and Roger, throwing stones at Henry, 'aimed to miss'.

With Bill, Roger, Sam and Eric watching, Jack begins to paint his face. When he finishes, the mask liberates him from 'shame and self-consciousness' and compels the boys to join him in the hunt.

Ralph, Piggy, Simon and Maurice are on the beach. Ralph sees a ship on the horizon and realises that there is no signal smoke from their fire – the hunters' responsibility. They discover that 'The fire was dead.' In cold fury Ralph sees the choir, chanting as they move up the beach, elatedly carrying a dead pig. Ralph confronts Jack, but caught up in the joy of describing the hunt, Ralph's message is ignored. Piggy joins in and Jack hits him, shattering one lens of his glasses. Jack apologises for the fire, which the hunters see as 'handsome behaviour' and which Ralph views as a 'verbal trick'.

The boys rebuild the fire and Ralph asserts his leadership by respectfully taking Piggy's glasses and relighting it – signalling that Ralph no longer needs to act alongside Jack. The boys cook the meat and the hunters begin to re-enact the hunt. Ralph, still angry, asserts his leadership and calls an assembly.

DEFINE IT!

mirage – optical illusion

sundial – clock that uses shadows to show the passing of time

DO IT!

As Ralph discovers there is no smoke from the fire, Golding presents an image of Henry and Johnny throwing sand at Percival. Why does Golding include this detail?

21

Savagery: 'The mask compelled them.'

Jack's action of painting his face is important. It is first mentioned by Jack in Chapter Three, when he sees a painted face as enabling him to camouflage himself, 'steal up on one – paint our faces so they wouldn't see'. By Chapter Four, the painted face has taken a more sinister turn. At the start, he states that it is 'Like in the war…dazzle paint.' Then the act of painting takes on the form of ritual, as Jack 'planned his new face' and kneels to apply the paint. Once complete, he is 'no longer himself but…an awesome stranger'. The effect of this 'drew the eyes of' Roger, Bill and Sam and Eric 'and appalled them'. Jack begins to 'dance' and his laughter changes to a 'bloodthirsty snarling'. Golding's use of 'bloodthirsty' here **foreshadows** the hunt that will soon happen.

The mask becomes 'a thing on its own', where Jack is 'liberated from shame and self-consciousness'. It is this liberation that enables Jack to become the ruthless dictator in the later chapters. He is removed from any personal responsibility for his actions through the mask. Similarly, the mask 'compels' the boys to follow him, to 'creep up and stab' – the very action that Jack could not perform in the first chapter.

Look at this extract from a student's answer to the question: 'How does Golding present the growing savagery of the boys?'

In Chapter Four, Golding builds the growing savagery in layers as he carefully shows the reader how the boys are shedding civilisation and the 'taboo of the old life'. Golding presents Maurice being aware of a telling-off for filling someone's eye with sand 'in his other life.' The repeated link to a life before the island and their acts of cruelty reinforces how civilisation is a very thin layer. In the same way that they shed clothes, they also shed their kindness, decency and their sense of society.

DO IT!

Continue this answer with details of the first successful hunt and what this shows us about the descent into savagery (from 'I got you meat!' to 'I'm calling an assembly.').

STRETCH IT!

Jack 'twitches' as he tells Ralph about the blood. Why does Golding include this detail?

Golding's methods

The kill: 'they had outwitted a living thing'

If your mind is 'crowded with memories', you could expect these memories to be positive; here they are filled with the savagery of the kill, and Jack glories in this kill.

'closed in' suggests that the boys were hunting as a pack of animals. The pig is 'struggling' – it is powerless and defenceless. The boys have no mercy.

> His mind was crowded with memories; memories of the knowledge that had come to them when they closed in on the struggling pig, knowledge that they had outwitted a living thing, imposed their will upon it, taken away its life like a long satisfying drink.

The boys have outsmarted the animal.

This suggests domination and lust for power – almost like the cruelty shown to the littluns by Roger.

This simile suggests they are feasting on the pig in the same way they will gorge on its flesh later in the chapter; 'long satisfying drink' links to their thirst for the kill – it is only satisfied by this violence.

Ralph and Jack are presented as opposites. They are facing each other like opponents and their worlds and obsessions have no connection. Notice that Ralph's common sense is 'baffled', he has no understanding of Jack's obsession with hunting. Instead, he is presented as 'longing' – yearning for rescue and shelter.

> The two boys faced each other. There was the brilliant world of hunting, tactics, fierce exhilaration, skill; and there was the world of longing and baffled common-sense.

Here, Simon represents the forces of good. He is presented as standing alone on the 'mountain-top' separate from the group. This metaphor shows 'Passions', anger and outrage, as wings – but as 'awful' wings, suggesting dread and terror.

> Passions beat about Simon on the mountain-top with awful wings.

DO IT!

Golding tells us that Ralph 'asserts his chieftainship' over Jack. What does he do to achieve this?

Character and theme essentials

Form: the island as a microcosm of the real world

The island can be seen to represent the world. This is called a 'microcosm', where places, situations, and communities are seen to represent in miniature different aspects of our world and society. Golding presents the boys as representing big ideas and concepts. Ralph represents democracy and civilisation whereas Jack represents the opposing concepts of dictatorship and lust for power. (See page 81 for further discussion of **allegory**.)

Theme: civilisation versus savagery

The first four chapters show the boys moving step by step away from civilisation and the rules they previously conformed to. Golding presents this through the shedding of their school and choir uniforms. Jack's mask and the boys' primitive chant, 'Kill the pig. Cut her throat. Spill her blood' and their dancing and laughter when talking about the blood during the kill all unite to show their loss of civilisation. Jack has moved from wanting to hunt to feed the boys to wanting to hunt for the kill itself. This is all by the end of Chapter Four. The reader wonders how much further they will descend by the end of the novel.

Context

Lord of the Flies was published in 1954, a time very close to the Second World War. Golding had fought in the war, and his experience influenced how he felt about human nature. When the novel was published, Golding's readers would have understood these experiences. They would have recognised the similarities between the fires on the island and the fires during the war. They would have recognised the references to the atom bomb. Social attitudes change throughout history and readers change too. This is what we mean by **context**: the circumstances that explain the **tone** and ideas in a novel. We need to consider how far the novel's messages about human nature are still relevant to our lives, beliefs and experiences today.

NAIL IT!

Use the novel's context to help you write meaningfully about the key element in your exam question. Focus on understanding:

- your own reaction to the text

- why you think that Golding wants the reader to respond in this way

- what Golding was trying to say about his own society.

Avoid making links to Golding's life.

REVIEW IT!

1 Which character opens the novel?

2 What item of clothing is Piggy wearing?

3 How does Golding show that Piggy is a different class to the rest of the boys?

4 Why is Ralph right when he says that the island 'a good island'?

5 Who tells Ralph how to blow the conch?

6 Find a quotation to show that Ralph and Jack can be successful when they work together.

7 Which boy first mentions the 'beastie', the 'snake-thing'?

8 What makes Ralph feel so certain they will be rescued?

9 When Ralph mentions the need for fire in Chapter Two, what happens?

10 How do the boys light the fire?

11 When the fire rages out of control, what home truths does Piggy tell the boys?

12 What happens as a result of the fire?

13 At the start of Chapter Three, Jack is hunting and Ralph is building shelters. How are their outcomes similar?

14 What has become taboo for the boys by Chapter Three?

15 How do Simon and Roger each treat the littluns?

16 How does Percival behave at the start of Chapter Four?

17 How do Piggy's glasses get broken?

18 Why is Ralph so angry when Jack apologises for letting the fire go out?

19 When Jack refuses to give Piggy meat, who gives Piggy his share?

20 Explain the difference between the way Ralph takes Piggy's glasses and the way Jack takes Piggy's glasses. What does this tell us about the two boys and what they stand for?

Chapters Five, Six, Seven and Eight

Chapter Five: Beast from Water

Summary

Ralph is heading towards the platform. Ralph considers leadership and wishes that he could think like Piggy – he is beginning to see Piggy's value.

Ralph blows the conch and the boys begin to appear. Ralph begins to outline what needs to be done. He talks about water, shelter and using only one place as a lavatory. The boys giggle and laugh at this. Ralph's final point is about the fire. He states they must have fire 'or die', then makes the rule of no fires anywhere other than on the mountain. He states they used to have fun before 'people began to get frightened' though he says he thinks it is 'nonsense'. He puts down the conch 'ceremonially' and Jack takes it up.

Jack begins by telling the boys they are 'cry-babies and sissies' before saying that they are all frightened and they will just have to 'put up with it'. He tells them that 'there is no beast in the forest'. Piggy states there is 'no fear' unless they 'get frightened of people'. A littlun called Phil comes forward to speak. He says he saw something 'big and horrid' in the trees. Simon admits it was him. He tries to articulate what he thinks the beast is, '…maybe it's only us'.

Percival comes forward and after some coaxing says that 'the beast comes out of the sea'. The meeting begins to break down. It is now almost dark and the talk has turned to ghosts. Ralph, seeing the breakdown of order, decides to call a vote on ghosts. There is a 'tussle' between Piggy and Jack where Jack ignores the conch before challenging Ralph and his rules. Jack leaps off with the boys to 'hunt down' the beast, leaving Piggy, Ralph and Simon.

Piggy tells Ralph to blow the conch, but Ralph knows that if he did, and the boys ignored it, everything would be lost. Simon tells Ralph that he should 'Go on being chief.' Piggy talks about Jack saying that he hates both Ralph and himself. The boys wish that adults would send a 'sign'. Percival, asleep, wails out in the darkness.

DEFINE IT!

debaters – speakers able to put forward a formal argument

effigy – figure/statue

ineffectual – unsuccessful

sough – rustling noise

tussle – scuffle

DO IT!

Golding describes the 'place of assembly' (paragraph beginning 'The place of assembly in which he stood…'). Make a list of the key features of this place or draw a labelled diagram.

Ralph's leadership: 'only here could he allow his feet to move without having to watch them'

In this chapter, we see how Ralph's leadership has grown. He has learned that silence is a means of controlling Jack, but he has also learned that leadership is 'an improvisation' and how life is 'spent watching one's feet'. Golding presents us with the leader who thinks about his actions – unlike the leader who reacts to events. Here, Ralph is second-guessing every decision he makes rather than leaping into action like Jack. This is the essential difference between them.

Ralph sets out his manifesto for leadership in this chapter. This is a manifesto of following rules that will benefit society, not the high excitement of 'tactics' and hunting but instead the rules of building shelters, ensuring hygienic living and working towards rescue. When he faces the challenge from Jack, both towards his leadership and towards the conch, the symbol of order and civilisation, he knows that if he blows the conch and the boys fail to react, all hope is lost. He knows that he cannot do this, despite urging from Piggy, the voice of reason.

It is at this point of the novel that Ralph learns the true value of Piggy. He has to 'adjust his values' and realises that Piggy 'for all his ludicrous body, had brains'. In Chapter Four, he takes the glasses from Piggy with respect in order to light the fire, unlike Jack who takes them with violence. Here, Ralph, Simon and Piggy can talk as equals as they discuss their desire for an adult to send them a 'sign' as they strive 'unsuccessfully to convey the majesty of adult life'.

DO IT!

Ralph says to Jack, 'the rules are the only thing we've got!' What does he mean?

Percival Wemys Madison

Percival is used by Golding to show the impact of the loss of civilisation and the end of innocence. Percival has been taught his name and address but at this point in the novel he can no longer remember his telephone number, 'telephone, telephone, tele –'; the thin layer of civilisation is breaking away. Percival represents innocence. His uncontrollable weeping and 'thin wail out of the darkness chilled them and set them grabbing for each other'. The outside world is 'powerless' to save him in this new, harsh world.

AQA exam-style question

How does Golding use events in *Lord of the Flies* to explore ideas about society?

Write about:

- some of the events in the book

- how Golding uses these events to explore ideas about society.

[30 marks]

The beast: 'maybe it's only us'

In an essay published in 1965, discussing the influence of the Second World War on the novel, Golding said: 'I had discovered what one man could do to another...I must say that anyone who moved through those years without understanding that man produces evil as a bee produces honey, must have been blind or wrong in the head...'

In Chapter Five, Golding presents both Piggy and Simon trying to explain that there is no physical beast. Piggy explains this from a scientific point of view that is later picked up by Maurice. He states there is no beast 'with claws and all that' and goes on to state that there is no fear either, 'Unless we get frightened of people.' Piggy, like Golding, knows that it is people who will 'produce evil as a bee produces honey', not any external being. Simon takes this further by telling the assembly that 'maybe there is a beast'. He makes the evil a reality, shocking both Ralph and Piggy, while clarifying that it is a reality because 'maybe it's only us'. However, Simon becomes 'inarticulate' and cannot explain his message of the evil contained within us all.

Jack uses the boys' fear of the beast to build his own power. Their fear weakens the group and by showing his strength through his hunting, he is able to impress the boys and give them a sense of security. It is in this section that Jack makes his first outright challenge of Ralph's authority, his rules and the symbolic power of the conch. Throughout the assembly he dismisses the beast, saying that 'There aren't any beasts to be afraid of on the island', shortly before declaring that 'we'll hunt it down' as he leads the boys to the beach for this hunt.

DO IT!

Look at these quotations about the beast:

> " I saw something big and horrid moving in the trees "

> " the beast comes out of the sea "

Now look at this description of the boys on the beach after they have left the platform:

> " The dispersed figures had come together on the sand and were a dense black mass that revolved. "

Why does Golding include this description of the boys on the beach?

STRETCH IT!

Ralph describes Simon, Piggy and himself as 'three blind mice'. Why does Golding use this reference?

Chapter Six: Beast from Air

Summary

The boys go to bed. Over the horizon there comes the result from a 'battle fought at ten miles' height'. There is an explosion and a 'figure' with 'dangling limbs' dropping below a parachute. This is a sign from the world of grown-ups.

Sam and Eric are trying to light the fire. They talk about Ralph's anger during the assembly and think about a schoolmaster's anger in their previous life. They see the parachute and airman and flee in terror. Ralph is dreaming of home and 'feeding the ponies with sugar'. The twins wake Ralph telling him what they saw. Ralph calls an assembly and Sam and Eric tell the boys who react in 'horror'. It is Jack who takes charge by calling them 'back to the centre'. Piggy suggests staying where they are instead of going to find the beast. Jack's contempt of Piggy and frustration with Ralph results in him rejecting the rule of the conch and declaring, 'We know who ought to say things.' Jack and Ralph end up in a power struggle as the boys watch 'intently'. Ralph reasserts control and the boys set off for the 'tail-end part' of the island with spears.

Simon knows there is no beast but knows within 'his inward sight' that humankind can be both 'heroic and sick'. The boys reach the 'castle' and Ralph takes charge, telling a hesitant Jack, 'I'm chief. I'll go. Don't argue.' Ralph is afraid, but once alone he realises that he will not 'meet any beast'. Jack joins him. Telling him, 'Couldn't let you do it on your own', the two boys regain some of their earlier friendship as they explore. Both Ralph and Jack know there is no beast, but they know that the other boys need their confirmation of this.

The other boys are excitedly pushing rocks into the sea when Ralph realises that the fire has gone out. The boys do not want to help but in the end do what he wants, 'mutinously'. Jack leads the way to relight the fire.

Golding's methods

Language of beauty and horror: 'bowed and sank and bowed again'

The 'sign' that arrives from the adult world is the dead pilot whose parachute is caught by the breeze as he falls to the island. In this description at the start of the chapter, Golding uses language to show the beauty of the scene, leaving the reader to imagine the horror of the dead body.

Look at these details from Golding's description of the scene:

> This is a gentle breeze suggesting playfulness.

> Colours are used to show the landscape's beauty. Flowers are associated with delicacy and fragility.

> " Yard by yard, puff by puff, the breeze hauled the figure through the blue flowers, over the boulders and red stones…Here the breeze was fitful and allowed the strings of the parachute to tangle and festoon; and the figure sat, its helmeted head between its knees, held by a complication of lines. When the breeze blew the lines would strain taut and some accident of this pull lifted the head and chest upright… "

> The figure 'sat', suggesting rest and tranquillity. Instead of using 'dead-body' or 'corpse', Golding refers to the dead pilot as the 'figure'. This distances the reader from the horror.

> The lines of the parachute 'festoon', suggesting they are like garlands, decoration.

However, the figure is 'hauled' through the flowers, suggesting a forcible dragging of the dead body. The final image here is the corpse's head lifting 'upright'. Golding presents the dignity of the figure as it 'sat' on the 'mountain-top', but the horror of the scene – especially when the reader considers that it will be young children who find the body – is shocking.

DO IT!

Look at this sentence:

> " So as the stars moved across the sky, the figure sat on the mountain-top and bowed and sank and bowed again. "

What methods does Golding use to suggest this movement will continue forever?

 STRETCH IT!

To get the highest marks in your AQA exam, you need to explore detailed links between different parts of the novel. What other episode from the novel might you choose to show Golding's use of beautiful images within a horrific scene?

Leadership

Jack: 'This is a hunter's job.'

Once again, in this chapter we see Ralph and Jack clash as Jack challenges Ralph's leadership. We see him sneer at Ralph, asking Ralph in front of the assembly if he is, 'Frightened'. On the positive side, it is Jack who calls the boys back from their alarm and stops the assembly disintegrating through terror.

Perhaps for the reader it is when Jack shouts, 'we don't need the conch any more', that we recognise the voice of a dictator. Here, he questions the value of others speaking: 'What good did Simon do speaking, or Bill or Walter?' and therefore by this means of silencing dissenting voices, 'deciding things' can be left to 'the rest of us'.

We have seen this autocratic approach from Jack before, in his military treatment of the choir in the opening chapter and his prejudice against Piggy. Jack represents the dictator. He wants rules but only when it suits him. In this case with the conch, he brushes it off as not needed. He enjoys the authority to punish when rules are broken.

 AQA exam-style question

How does Golding present Ralph as a leader in *Lord of the Flies*?

Write about:

- how Ralph reacts as a leader

- how Golding presents Ralph by the way he writes.

[30 marks]

Here is a student's first outline plan for their response to this question. Add an extra bullet point for each assessment objective (AO).

Response to task and text (AO1)

- Why Ralph is elected as chief - his looks and charisma, 'A stillness that marked him out' and the conch.

- Reactions to Ralph as he tries to get the boys to work towards rescue and shelter, e.g. Jack's challenges, the boys' need for the instant gratification of play rather than long-term goals.

-

Identification of writer's methods (AO2)

- The reader is closest to Ralph - we know more of his thought processes and concerns.

- Use and effects of hesitancy, dashes to suggest his inability to think under pressure, e.g. 'We'd have given them fire for themselves only they stole it. '; 'He paused lamely as the curtain flickered in his brain.' (Chapter Eleven)

-

Understanding of ideas/perspectives/contexts (AO3)

- Treatment of the idea of civilisation, e.g. how Ralph's focus on rescue and safety cannot compete with the excitement of hunting.

-

DEFINE IT!

boar – a male pig with tusks

covert – here, a dense group of bushes or trees

ritually – in a ceremony

Chapter Seven: Shadows and Tall Trees

Summary

The boys are following along the pig run towards the mountain. It is hot. Ralph considers washing his shirt and cutting his hair. He realises how dirty all of the boys are, but more importantly, realises that he has stopped noticing. He watches the sea and feels despair in the face of their helplessness, 'This was the divider, the barrier.' Simon comes to talk to Ralph and makes a prediction that 'You'll get back to where you came from.'

The boys are frightened but Ralph is comfortable that Jack is in charge of the hunt. He thinks of memories of home, before he had been 'sent away to school'. Suddenly a boar appears and Ralph finds he 'was able to measure the distance coldly and take aim'. Ralph is caught up in the hunt and how his 'spear stuck in a bit'. He notices the 'new respect' he receives and 'felt that hunting was good after all'. Jack shows the boys a 'rip' on his arm and attention returns to him.

The boys begin to re-enact the ritual of the kill and Ralph joins in. Robert plays the part of the pig but as things change from play to 'frenzy' Robert squeals in 'real pain'. Jack has Robert by the hair, 'brandishing his knife', as the 'chant rose ritually'. Even Ralph wanted to 'get a handful' of 'brown, vulnerable flesh'. The ritual stops and Ralph uneasily states that it was 'Just a game.'

The boys discuss whether to go back to Piggy or go to the mountain. Simon volunteers to go through the forest alone to tell Piggy where they are. As they make their way to the mountain, boys begin to drop out. Ralph and Jack, involved in a power struggle, continue with Roger. Jack goes up to the top but returns, frightened, saying he saw something 'bulge'. Ralph takes charge and leads towards the top with Roger 'lagging a little'. Despite his fear, Ralph steps forwards. He sees 'something like a great ape'. The boys run, leaving their sharpened sticks behind.

DO IT!

Why do you think Ralph is happy to let Jack lead the way in this chapter?

Savagery: 'The desire to squeeze and hurt was over-mastering.'

Up until this point in the novel, Ralph has remained 'baffled' by Jack's obsession with the kill. Ralph begins to understand the excitement of hunting: Golding presents him taking on the hunter's role, discovering he is able to measure the distance to the fleeing animal 'coldly'.

After the boar escapes, the boys re-enact the hunt. Golding shows the reader just how thin the layer of civilisation is within the boys – even Ralph – as the 'play' becomes real. We are shown the level of Robert's fear as he 'blundered among them' being hit and 'jabbed' with spears. We are shown Robert 'screaming and struggling' with the strength of the 'frenzy'. 'Frenzy' suggests wild excitement that is out of control. This takes a further chilling turn as the boys begin the chant the reader recognises from when they killed the pig: 'Kill the pig! Cut his throat! Bash him in!' Even the voice of society and civilisation, Ralph, was 'fighting' to grab handfuls of the 'vulnerable' flesh. Golding's use of 'fighting' and 'vulnerable' here powerfully shows the violence of the ritual and Robert/the pig's powerlessness.

In the aftermath of the 'kill', the boys discuss how to develop the ritual.

Here are the details they suggest:

- adding a drum
- adding fire
- someone dressing up as a pig
- adding a real pig to kill
- using a littlun instead of a pig.

These additions show us a society that now accepts primitive rituals to share the experience of the hunt within their community. This ritual involves re-enactment, chanting and dancing already. The boys propose adding drum music, fire and animal sacrifice. Jack's final joke about using a 'littlun', with the associated taboo of child sacrifice, suggests the dark possible future of their savagery.

Golding presents Ralph's memories of his childhood home just before this savage scene. What message does Golding want the reader to understand here?

NAIL IT!

Make links between events throughout the novel to show your understanding of Golding's ideas, **themes** and message.

STRETCH IT!

How does this list foreshadow later events in the novel?

Simon: 'You're batty.'

It is in this chapter that Simon tells Ralph, 'You'll get back to where you came from.' This seemingly simple statement raises three questions. Does it mean that Ralph will be rescued? Does it mean that Ralph will regain his status amongst the boys? Why doesn't Simon say 'we' to suggest that he will return too?

Golding presents Simon as questioning whether Sam and Eric had truly seen the beast in Chapter Six. With a 'flicker of incredulity' he thinks of the questions that hadn't even occurred to Piggy, the voice of reason: why was this ferocious beast 'not fast enough to catch Samneric'? Simon is unafraid to go through the jungle on his own towards nightfall to tell Piggy that the boys will be back later. He spends time alone in the jungle, so it holds no fear for him. However, he also knows that there is no beast other than the beast within them all.

The beast from air: 'great ape'

The dead airman represents the war within the adult world that is mirrored by the boys on the island. On the island, this figure is the first physical indication that the beast is real, a physical being. This discovery accelerates the descent into savagery that leads to the violence and terror at the end of the novel. Golding presents this creature as a 'great ape' connecting a primitive version of humankind with this demonstration of the beast and Simon's knowledge that the beast is within us all.

When Ralph heads towards the top of the mountain, Jack asks him if he is 'scared'. Ralph is described as, 'Not scared as much as paralysed; hung up here immovable on the top of the diminishing, moving mountain.' Ralph, like the pilot, is caught in a situation that is making 'creatures' of them all.

 DO IT!

How does Golding present Roger in this chapter? Write a paragraph to explain your ideas.

 AQA exam-style question

'Some characters in *Lord of the Flies* suffer because they are different from most of the other boys on the island.'

How does Golding present the effects of being different in this society?

Write about:

• what characters who are different say and do

• how Golding presents the effects of being different.

[30 marks]

Chapter Eight: Gift for the Darkness

Summary

Back on the beach, Ralph tells Piggy that he saw the beast. When Ralph calls the hunters 'Boys armed with sticks', Jack storms off and blows the conch. Jack begins to manipulate the boys against Ralph, finally asking them to vote against him being chief. When the boys won't, Jack leaves in tears, telling the boys that they can join him if they wish.

Ralph tells Piggy that he is sure Jack will 'come back'. Simon says that they ought to climb the mountain. Piggy, more assured without Jack, suggests moving the fire from the top of the mountain to the beach. The boys build the fire and Piggy lights it. Ralph realises that the fire was hard to build because there were so few 'biguns'. Maurice, Bill and Roger have left.

Jack, 'brilliantly happy', declares they will 'forget the beast' and focus on hunting. The boys go to hunt and they come across a sow feeding her piglets. A violent hunt takes place, where Roger thrusts his spear 'Right up her ass' and Jack cuts her throat. Roger realises that they will need fire and Jack says they will 'paint' their faces, 'raid them and take fire'. Jack spears the sow's head on a sharpened stick as an offering to the beast.

In his place in the jungle, Simon sees the sow's head and begins to hallucinate. Ralph and Piggy realise that 'Samneric' have gone. The hunters – 'Demoniac figures' – arrive to raid the fire and Jack shouts that the boys can ask to join his hunters before inviting them to the feast. Simon, as part of his hallucination, talks to the head on the stick, the 'Lord of the Flies'. The head tells him that the beast isn't 'something that you can hunt and kill', instead, that it's 'part of you'. It finally tells Simon, 'we shall do you. See?' before listing the boys involved. Simon loses consciousness.

DO IT!

Write a paragraph to explain how Jack tries to manipulate the boys before he leaves 'Ralph's lot'.

DEFINE IT!

demoniac – like demons, evil creatures from hell

Lord of the Flies – Beelzebub, a demon or sometimes the Devil

waxy – slang for cross or angry

The hunt: 'full of sweat and noise and blood and terror'

The hunt, Jack's first act as newly declared chief, shows the boys' descent into savagery and foreshadows the violence that will escalate in the final chapters. In these chapters, the violence moves from hunting pigs for meat to hunting or killing other boys for the joy of violence and cruelty itself.

In this hunt, Golding begins to reveal the thrill the boys receive through the killing of the sow. The violence is hard-hitting, especially when the reader considers that this is a sow that they discover in 'deep maternal bliss' with her 'row of piglets that slept or burrowed or squeaked'. Notice the quiet of this idyllic scene that is about to be shattered. There was 'no wind'; Jack is 'silent'; the hunters inch forward in the 'silence and the heat'. This silence is broken by one word: 'Now!' and a cacophony of noise begins.

Look at this student's response:

> Golding immerses the reader into the hunt's war-like noise. We hear a 'demented shriek', showing the madness and chaos of the scene. However, this noise comes from a 'piglet' disturbed as it was feeding from its mother. Here Golding reinforces the savagery of the hunters, before following this with the 'gasping squeal' of the mother.

DO IT!

As the hunt continues, Golding uses contrasts between the beauty of the island and the violence of the hunt. Find three examples of both beauty and horror in this scene. Why do you think Golding uses these contrasts?

Killing the sow: 'terrified squealing became a high-pitched scream'

As the sow falls to the ground, the hunters 'fall on her'. Jack is 'on top of the sow' and Roger begins to push his spear 'inch by inch' into her anus. Here the sow gives a 'high-pitched scream', a human sound and the 'hot blood' spouts over Jack's hands. Golding tells the reader that the boys were 'heavy and fulfilled upon her'. This nightmarish, sexually charged scene, shows the depth of the boys' savagery. Their primitive belief in the beast, becoming real as they witness the airman, strips them of any remaining civility.

STRETCH IT!

Is it important that it is a sow rather than a boar that the boys kill at this point in the novel? Explain your ideas.

Jack as chief: 'I'm not going to play any longer. Not with you.'

After fleeing tearfully from the vote, we next see Jack 'standing before a small group of boys'. Golding tells us he is 'brilliantly happy'. Here we see Jack as an autocratic leader (someone who has full power and control and who makes all decisions for the group):

- Jack tells the boys that he will be chief – there are no votes this time.
- Jack tells the boys what they should believe: they are 'going to forget the beast'.
- Jack establishes rituals: 'We'll kill a pig and give a feast.'
- The boys follow him 'obediently'.
- Jack assumes the name/title 'Chief'.
- Jack establishes that they will 'put on paint' when they go to raid the fire.
- Jack establishes religious rituals of leaving an offering for the beast and sharpening 'a stick at both ends'.
- Jack presents himself as a god-like 'garlanded' idol.
- Jack establishes that he has the power to let them join his tribe, or not – he alone makes decisions.
- Jack establishes the chant: 'The Chief has spoken' after each of his statements.
- Jack's name has become taboo for anyone outside the group – Ralph's lot.

DO IT!

Golding tells us, 'The silence accepted the gift and awed them.' What does he mean by this?

Simon and the 'Lord of the Flies'

The head on the stick is covered with flies, a grotesque and sickening image. The 'Lord of the Flies' tells Simon that there is no one to help him, so Simon is alone with the knowledge that the beast is 'part of you'. The head uses the voice of 'a schoolmaster' inspiring fear, but it uses Jack's words, 'We are going to have fun on this island.' These words take on a menacing tone as Jack's type of 'fun' is made clear in this chapter. Golding reinforces this by foreshadowing Simon's death, 'we shall do you', and listing who will be involved: 'Jack and Roger and Maurice and Robert and Bill and Piggy and Ralph.' This list, held together by 'and', becomes a child-like chant that mirrors the ritualistic chant of the hunters. Notice that 'Ralph' is at the end of the list.

Character and theme essentials

Civilisation versus savagery

In Chapters Five to Eight, the breakdown of civilisation speeds up until the boys – under Jack's influence – begin to focus on the thrill of killing more than the function of the kill to get meat for food. Rituals develop surrounding the kill: the dance, the chant 'Kill the pig…' and then the re-enactment with one of the boys taking the role of the pig. A sacrifice of a pig – or jokingly a littlun – is also suggested for the future. By Chapter Eight, these rituals take on further primitive traits as an offering is made to the beast after the kill.

Fear

The boys' growing fear on the island develops into a primitive belief system. Here we see rituals developing as well as taboo subjects. 'Snakes' and the 'beast' become taboo words just as 'Jack' becomes taboo for Piggy and Ralph once Jack splits away from the group.

Power

Ralph and Jack

In Chapter Seven, we see Ralph learning how to challenge Jack once again. He has already defeated him through the power of silence in Chapter Four, but here we see him challenging Jack 'out of the new understanding that Piggy had given him'. Once again, we see Piggy in the role of adviser to the leader, the voice of intellect and reason. His insight that 'he hates you too, Ralph' (Chapter Five) prompts Ralph to challenge Jack asking, 'Why do you hate me?' Jack cannot answer and the boys are uncomfortable: they stir 'uneasily, as though something indecent had been said'.

Symbols

A pig's head on a stick

The pig's head refers to itself as 'Lord of the Flies'. In Christian sources, this refers to Beelzebub, another name for the Devil. In the Testament of Solomon, a text associated with the Old Testament in the Bible, Beelzebub will cause jealousy and murders and bring on war.

The conch

As a symbol of order and civilisation, it does not surprise the reader that Jack has no interest in the conch when he splits from 'Ralph's lot' – despite Piggy's fear. As an autocratic leader, he will control who will speak and even what they say, so he has no need for such a device. Notice how he blows the conch 'inexpertly' when he calls an assembly in Chapter Eight and Ralph soon takes it from him.

REVIEW IT!

1 Whose thoughts are described as 'a maze of thoughts that were rendered vague by his lack of words to express them'?

2 Who is described as having 'a ludicrous body', but also brains?

3 What 'practical business' has Ralph learned about addressing an assembly?

4 Why is Piggy scared that Ralph will give up being chief in Chapter Five?

5 What device does Golding use when he presents Piggy saying 'We'd be here until we died'?

6 Ralph asks the adult world for a sign. How is this answered?

7 Who flees from the beast with 'one terrified mind between them'?

8 At night, what does Ralph dream about?

9 Who says, 'We know who ought to say things'?

10 When Jack joins Ralph as he goes to the top of the mountain to see the beast, what does he say?

11 In Chapter Seven, Ralph notices how dirty the boys are. Why does Golding include this detail?

12 What prediction does Simon make about Ralph? Why does Golding include this?

13 The boys re-enact killing the pig in Chapter Seven. How does this link to the theme of savagery?

14 Simon is happy to go through the forest alone. Why is this?

15 Roger goes up the mountain with Ralph and Jack. Why is this surprising?

16 When Ralph tells Piggy about the beast in Chapter Eight, Piggy is surprised. What does this tell the reader about Piggy?

17 When Jack calls a vote to say whether Ralph should be chief, what happens?

18 How does Piggy change after Jack leaves the group?

19 How will Jack make fire without Piggy's glasses?

20 What does the 'Lord of the Flies' tell Simon?

Chapter Nine: A View to a Death

Summary

The weather is building towards a storm. Simon wakes following his fit. He crawls out of the space asking, 'What else is there to do?' As he looks up to the mountain top, he sees a 'humped thing suddenly sit on the top and look down at him'. Simon understands what this figure is. Simon is sick but frees the figure – symbolically freeing the boys from their fear. Simon knows the beast is 'harmless and horrible' and knows that he must share this news 'as soon as possible'.

The weather continues to build. Ralph and Piggy are bathing. They realise that everyone else is at Jack's party and Piggy suggests they should go too. As they approach, they find Jack sitting 'painted and garlanded' like an 'idol'. Piggy is accidentally hurt, breaking the tension as the boys laugh. Jack continues to behave like a ruler, issuing orders to control both the boys and the food.

Ralph, trying to assert his leadership, says he has the conch. Jack denies both Ralph's leadership and the conch, saying that it 'doesn't count at this end of the island'. Ralph realises the boys will have no shelter in the storm and Piggy advises that they leave as 'There's going to be trouble.' Jack's answer is for the boys to begin 'our dance'. During the dance with Roger as the pig, Piggy and Ralph join in. The chant's 'steady pulse' begins and 'another desire' rises, 'thick, urgent, blind'. The storm breaks and a 'thing' crawls out of the forest. Simon cries out about 'a dead man on the hill'. The 'beast' on its knees is in the centre of the circle, before breaking out on to the shore. The boys leap on it as they 'screamed, struck, bit, tore'.

The rain begins. Seeing 'what a small beast it is', at that moment, the boys run screaming as the wind takes the body of the airman from the mountain top out to sea.

Towards midnight, Simon's body, surrounded by light, is taken out to sea.

Golding's methods

Pathetic fallacy: 'Over the island the build-up of clouds continued.'

With the tension between the two groups of boys reaching a crisis point, coupled with their fear of the beast, Golding uses **pathetic fallacy** to reflect this storm of emotion. This storm finally breaks during the frenzied dance ('The dark sky was shattered by a blue-white scar.') and the re-enactment of the hunt.

DO IT!

Find a further example of pathetic fallacy in this chapter and annotate to explain Golding's methods.

NAIL IT!

To indicate that you are exploring possible interpretations, use tentative words such as 'perhaps', 'this could'/'might', 'suggest'/'imply'.

Look at this description from the chapter's opening:

This build-up is ongoing, 'steady' and relentless.

Suggesting the boys' tension and fear

The air is perhaps reflecting the boys' heightened emotions.

Violent, war-like image to imply that the air is at breaking point

> Over the island the build-up of clouds continued. A steady current of heated air rose all day from the mountain and was thrust to ten thousand feet; revolving masses of gas piled up the static until the air was ready to explode. By early evening the sun had gone and a brassy glare had taken the place of clear daylight. Even the air that pushed in from the sea was hot and held no refreshment. Colours drained from water and trees and pink surfaces of rock, and the white and brown clouds brooded.

Linked to 'steady' suggesting that the static is loaded, creating a jittery, pressurised mood

Like the harsh 'brassy' yellow colour, this light is unpleasantly hard and bright.

Suggesting the air is rudely making its way from the sea

The vibrant colours of the island are bleeding from the landscape.

Suggesting that the clouds are moping or in a fretful mood

41

Simon and the truth about the beast: 'What else is there to do?'

Simon bravely heads up alone to the top of the mountain, where the beast lies in wait. Notice that he had suggested this previously to Ralph. Golding presents Simon as freeing the dead airman literally, through his actions, and symbolically freeing the boys from their fear of the beast by releasing the parachute and body. As he makes his way back through the jungle, Simon is shown as bringing the truth to the boys. In doing this, Simon dies.

Golding's methods: Simon and the beast

As the boys chant and dance, look how the reader's focus shifts from Simon to the beast to the boys. Both the boys and Simon are dehumanised in this scene. Not only does Simon become the beast, but the frenzied boys merge to become one beast.

The focus is on the chant. The reader is familiar with this. The reader also knows how this can stir savage instincts in the boys as we remember Ralph's response to the chant.

Focus on Simon who has now been stripped of his humanity to become 'a thing'

Language suggesting that this is a creature – not human

Focus is back to Simon and the harsh blue–white lightning. Combined with the noise and the dance, Golding presents the drama of the scene almost as if in a film.

The noise is agonising, out of control.

The chant punctuates the scene. Notice the addition of 'Do him in!' foreshadowing the horror to come.

In their frenzied chanting, the boys too are animal-like.

Simile suggesting lack of control in the frenzy – perhaps foreshadowing the pain to come as a result of this

Simon's truth; a religious reference to the crucifixion of Christ on a hill

The boys, in their circle, now have a 'mouth'. They have become the beast as they 'crunched and screamed'.

> A thing was crawling out of the forest. It came darkly, uncertainly. The shrill screaming that rose before the beast was like a pain. The beast stumbled into the horseshoe.
>
> 'Kill the beast! Cut his throat! Spill his blood!'
>
> The blue-white scar was constant, the noise unendurable. Simon was crying out something about a dead man on a hill.
>
> 'Kill the beast! Cut his throat! Spill his blood! Do him in!'
>
> The sticks fell and the mouth of the new circle crunched and screamed. The beast was on its knees in the centre, its arms folded over its face.

Notice how vulnerable the 'beast' is, as shown by the kneeling position. The boys, as the beast, are now in control.

Golding describes this in a matter-of-fact way – he is a dispassionate observer of this savagery. It is also helpful to consider why he does not write this from the point of view of one of the boys.

Pronoun suggests inhumanity

A stark list of violent acts emphasising the inhuman savagery of the boys' actions

" At once the crowd surged after it, poured down the rock, leapt on to the beast, screamed, struck, bit, tore. There were no words, and no movements but the tearing of teeth and claws. "

The boys are moving as one fluid creature.

A description used previously about the beast

The death of Simon: 'The beast lay huddled on the pale beach'

Look at this student's response to Golding's use of light images after Simon dies. Notice how the student uses quotations and introduces contexts to reinforce their ideas:

As the storm calms and clears, Simon's body remains on the beach. Golding presents the scene visually with images of light suggesting heavenly light or candle-lit religious ceremonies. There are 'bright constellations' that are reflected by the 'clear water' and 'phosphorescence' bulges around the pebbles. Strange 'moonbeam-bodied creatures with fiery eyes' appear. These images of light and beauty contrast with Simon's 'broken body' that 'stains' the sand. Golding again points to Simon being different from the other boys - a spiritual being. This is emphasised as Simon is 'moved out towards the open sea.'

DOIT!

Look at the paragraph beginning 'Now a great wind blew the rain sideways' to 'and bumped it over the reef and out to sea'.

What happens step by step to:

• the airman?

• the boys?

 STRETCHIT!

Is the text describing the airman in the Do it! above beautiful or horrific? Write a paragraph to explain your ideas.

Chapter Ten: The Shell and the Glasses

Summary

Ralph and Piggy cannot discuss Simon's death. Ralph states, 'That was murder', but Piggy stops him before making excuses: 'It was dark. There was that – that bloody dance.' Ralph is prepared to admit that he wasn't scared but can't articulate how he felt. Piggy states that 'It was an accident', which soon shifts to 'He asked for it.' They decide they were on the outside and didn't see anything. Sam and Eric arrive, also uncomfortable. The boys cannot look each other in the eye. Sam and Eric claim they were 'very tired' so 'left early', despite their injuries. The 'Memory of the dance that none of them had attended' shook them all.

DEFINE IT!

bowstave – curved arc

At Castle Rock, sentries challenge Roger. The challenge is a new order from the 'Chief'. Roger is shown a loose rock that could be levered from the top of the cliff. The boys discuss how Jack is 'a proper Chief'. Robert tells Roger, 'He's going to beat Wilfred.' The boys don't know why. Jack, now referred to as 'the Chief' is sitting naked to the waist with his face 'blocked out' in white and red. Wilfred has been 'newly beaten'. Jack explains the need for defence against Ralph's lot who will 'try to spoil things'. He stokes fear about the beast saying that it came 'in disguise'. The boys realise that they cannot light the fire. Jack says they will go to get fire 'from the others'. Roger and Maurice volunteer to go with him.

Ralph, Piggy and Sam and Eric struggle to keep the fire going. Civilisation is fading in Ralph's memory. He knows that fire is good but cannot remember why. It is Piggy who explains that it's for rescue. The boys go to bed and Ralph begins his 'nightly game of supposing', thinking of home. Sam and Eric begin fighting each other. Piggy tells Ralph that if they don't go home soon they'll be 'barmy'.

DO IT!

Piggy thinks at first that Jack and the hunters had come for the conch. Explain why he would think this.

The boys hear something moving outside. A voice 'whispered horribly... Piggy – Piggy –'. Something crashes into the shelter and a savage fight begins. The fight wakes the littluns and Ralph tells them, 'We've had a fight with the others.' The boys discuss the fight, injuries received and given. Piggy was afraid that they wanted the conch. Jack and his hunters move across the beach carrying Piggy's glasses.

Power: 'The Chief'

During this chapter, Golding presents what happens when leaders have complete power over their subjects, through Jack's leadership. The last time we saw Jack's leadership was in Chapter Nine, when he was 'garlanded' like an 'idol' – presenting himself as a representation of a god. In this chapter, his leadership becomes even more extreme. Robert tells Roger that Wilfred is going to be 'beaten'. He does not know why, just that 'He [Jack] got angry.' When Roger finds Jack, he is 'naked to the waist' and has painted his face. The shedding of clothes and this use of paint symbolically represents the descent into savagery. Paint also enables the boys to hide from their mounting acts of savagery.

Golding now refers to Jack as 'the Chief' as do 'tribe' members. These boys have developed from the 'choir' to the 'hunters' to the 'tribe'; each renaming a step from civilisation towards savagery. Golding shows the Chief pointing at 'this savage and that with his spear'.

Golding shows Jack using strategies used by autocratic leaders to manipulate the tribe:

- He creates suspicion of 'others', those outside the tribe, by creating a need for guards at the gate 'so that others don't sneak in'.

- He amplifies this suspicion of 'others' by giving them motives, 'to try to spoil things we do'.

- He stokes fear of the beast by saying that the beast may try to come in.

- He plays on that fear (and plays down their role in killing Simon) by saying that the beast came in disguise and they cannot kill it.

- He creates a new religion/mythology surrounding the beast, creating taboo areas – 'leave the mountain alone' – and offerings to satisfy it – 'give it the head if you go hunting' – to develop their fear.

- He uses 'our dance' to bond them against their fear of the beast.

DO IT!

How do the boys react to Jack as chief?

AQA exam-style question

How does Golding use the character of Jack to explore ideas about power in *Lord of the Flies*?

Write about:

- what Jack says and does

- how Golding uses the character of Jack to explore ideas about power.

[30 marks]

45

Golding's methods

Building suspense: '...what am I going to do?'

After the fight, Golding builds suspense through the use of delayed information about the reason why Jack and his hunters raided the shelter.

Look how Golding structures the information given:

DO IT!

Look at the opening section of the chapter where Ralph, Piggy and Sam and Eric meet following Simon's death. Using the model (right), track Golding's presentation of the boys' discomfort. Begin with Ralph stating, 'That was murder' and end with, 'We left early.'

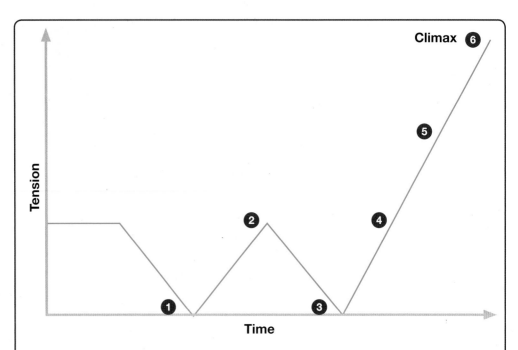

1 Sam and Eric, Piggy and Ralph discuss their injuries and the injuries they gave to Jack and his hunters. Following the tension after the fight, Golding quickly establishes that the boys are not badly injured. As this follows Simon's death, the reader has been worried for the boys' safety. Tension falls.

2 Piggy says he thought they wanted the conch. Golding supplies a motive for the attack. Tension rises.

3 Ralph establishes that the conch is still there. Golding has supplied a red herring. Tension falls.

4 Piggy says he knows that they didn't take the conch, before saying, 'They came for something else. Ralph – what am I going to do?' Golding uses vague language: 'something else'. He holds back the information of what else was taken. Tension rises.

5 The focus shifts to Jack, Roger and Maurice making their way to Castle Rock. The boys are 'singing', turning 'cartwheels' and Jack is 'exulting in his achievement'. Golding shifts the focus to the hunters. The filmic description of the boys' carefree movements contrasts with Ralph, Sam and Eric and Piggy. The reader questions why they are so happy. Tension rises.

6 The focus shifts to Jack's left hand: there 'dangled Piggy's broken glasses'. Like a camera, Golding zooms into the detail of Jack's left hand and the glasses. This adds to the shock of the information. Golding adds no comment to this visual image. Tension rises to a climax.

STRETCH IT!

Golding uses 'shrilly' twice in this chapter to describe Piggy's tone of voice. Why does he do this?

Chapter Eleven: Castle Rock

Summary

Ralph, Piggy and Sam and Eric cannot light the fire without the glasses and Piggy cannot see. Piggy instructs Ralph to blow the conch and call a meeting. Ralph cannot articulate his thoughts. After some prompting by Piggy, Ralph suggests that they 'smarten up a bit' and go to Jack. The boys discuss how they should dress. Eric is worried that Jack will be 'painted'. Ralph says they won't paint themselves 'because we aren't savages'.

They head to Castle Rock. As they reach it, a 'war-cry' is heard. Roger challenges them as the sentry. Ralph blows the conch. Piggy begs Ralph not to leave him. Roger throws a stone at Sam and Eric 'aiming to miss'.

Ralph declares he is calling an assembly. 'A painted face spoke with the voice of Robert' to tell them that Jack is hunting. At this, Jack appears with two painted hunters, carrying a headless pig. Jack tells Ralph to 'go away' and Ralph demands Piggy's specs. Ralph calls Jack a 'thief' and a fight begins between the two boys. Piggy reminds Ralph why they are there: 'The fire. My specs.' Ralph talks about rescue before calling the tribe, 'painted fools'. Jack orders Sam and Eric to be tied up. Ralph screams at Jack, 'You're a beast and a swine and a bloody, bloody thief!' causing Jack to charge. Piggy, holding the conch, calls to speak, surprising the tribe into silence. Roger, with one hand on the lever, throws stones at Ralph and Piggy.

Piggy tells them they are acting like 'a crowd of kids', Ralph and Jack begin yelling and Roger continues to drop stones. The tribe, a 'solid mass of menace' prepares to charge. Roger with 'delirious abandonment' leans his weight on the lever. The rock falls, hitting Piggy and smashing the conch. Piggy falls forty feet and lands on his back. 'His head opened' and his legs and arms 'twitched' before the sea takes his body away.

The silence is complete. Jack threatens Ralph, screaming 'That's what you'll get!' before hurling his spear at Ralph. Ralph runs. Jack begins questioning Sam before Roger advances to take over, 'wielding a nameless authority'.

DO IT!

Before they leave for Castle Rock, Piggy reminds Ralph about smoke for rescue and Ralph gets annoyed with him. The twins examine Ralph 'as though they were seeing him for the first time'. What does Golding mean here?

DEFINE IT!

delirious – excited, feverish

inscrutably – unreadable

myopia – short-sightedness

sabre – a curved sword

NAIL IT!

Moments that show
the clash between
savagery and
civilisation are key
events in the novel.
Pay close attention to
this chapter as it may
be useful in your exam.

Civilisation versus savagery: 'What's grown-ups goin' to think?

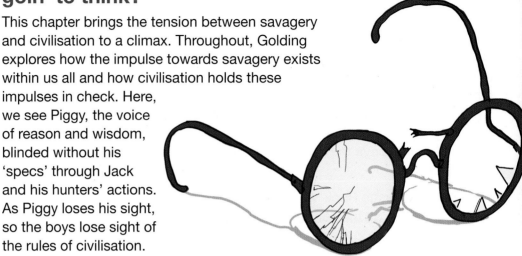

This chapter brings the tension between savagery
and civilisation to a climax. Throughout, Golding
explores how the impulse towards savagery exists
within us all and how civilisation holds these
impulses in check. Here,
we see Piggy, the voice
of reason and wisdom,
blinded without his
'specs' through Jack
and his hunters' actions.
As Piggy loses his sight,
so the boys lose sight of
the rules of civilisation.

Golding firstly reveals this impulse towards savagery through the clothes
and paint worn by the boys. When Piggy wants to go to Castle Rock at the
start of the chapter to retrieve his glasses, Ralph's thought is that they 'could
smarten up a bit and then go –' showing that Ralph, as in Chapter One, still
retains the conventions of 'the Home Counties', our society. Sam is scared
that Jack will 'be painted'; we see how far this has developed when they
reach Castle Rock and 'Savages' appear 'painted out of recognition'. The
boys are 'Freed by the paint' and the consequences of any actions through
their 'painted anonymity'. Ralph cannot remember 'what Jack looked like' as
Jack loses his humanity, transforming into 'the red and green mask'.

Golding presents this loss of humanity as a means of showing how the
'savages' view those outside the tribe. Roger, looking down on Piggy and
Ralph, drops stones down on them. Roger sees Ralph merely as 'a shock
of hair' and Piggy as 'a bag of fat'. Both Ralph and Piggy are reduced to a
single physical feature, stripping them of their humanity.

This loss of humanity is seen further as Golding links Piggy to a pig
throughout. When they arrive at Castle Rock, Piggy 'crouched, his back
shapeless as a sack'. When Jack arrives, there is the 'headless and
paunched body of a sow' lying on the grass 'where they had left it', mirroring
Piggy's position.

DO IT!

When Jack orders the
tribe to grab Sam and
Eric, how does Golding
present the twins'
reaction?

AQA exam-style question

How does Golding use Roger to explore ideas about human nature
in *Lord of the Flies*?

Write about:

• how Golding presents the character of Roger

• how Golding uses Roger to explore ideas about human nature.

[30 marks]

The Death of Piggy: 'This time the silence was complete.'

Piggy represents reason and intelligence on the island. We see him frequently referring to the adult world, talking about his 'auntie' and wondering what 'grown-ups' would think about their behaviour. In fact, it is a link to his auntie's neighbour that leads Piggy to tell Ralph how to blow the conch, the signal that brings the boys together and the symbol of order and civilisation. As Piggy dies, the conch is smashed with him. This signals how order and reason, like Piggy and the conch, will 'cease to exist' on the island.

DO IT!

When Piggy lands on the rock, Golding states: 'His head opened and stuff came out.' Why does Golding include this detail?

Golding presents the action unemotionally as a series of small events. This slows the pace, following the chaos and violence of the previous scene:

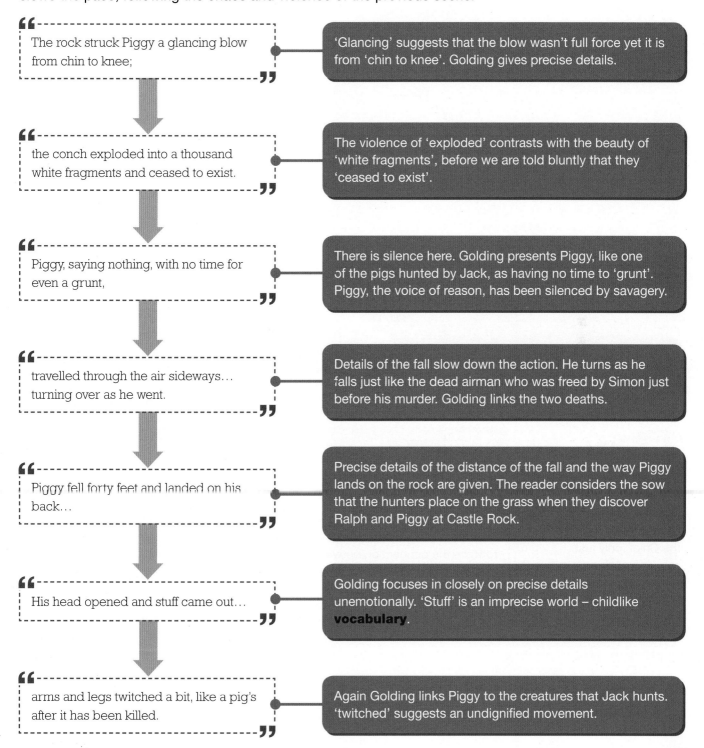

"The rock struck Piggy a glancing blow from chin to knee;"

'Glancing' suggests that the blow wasn't full force yet it is from 'chin to knee'. Golding gives precise details.

"the conch exploded into a thousand white fragments and ceased to exist."

The violence of 'exploded' contrasts with the beauty of 'white fragments', before we are told bluntly that they 'ceased to exist'.

"Piggy, saying nothing, with no time for even a grunt,"

There is silence here. Golding presents Piggy, like one of the pigs hunted by Jack, as having no time to 'grunt'. Piggy, the voice of reason, has been silenced by savagery.

"travelled through the air sideways... turning over as he went."

Details of the fall slow down the action. He turns as he falls just like the dead airman who was freed by Simon just before his murder. Golding links the two deaths.

"Piggy fell forty feet and landed on his back..."

Precise details of the distance of the fall and the way Piggy lands on the rock are given. The reader considers the sow that the hunters place on the grass when they discover Ralph and Piggy at Castle Rock.

"His head opened and stuff came out..."

Golding focuses in closely on precise details unemotionally. 'Stuff' is an imprecise world – childlike **vocabulary**.

"arms and legs twitched a bit, like a pig's after it has been killed."

Again Golding links Piggy to the creatures that Jack hunts. 'twitched' suggests an undignified movement.

Roger: 'The hangman's horror clung to him.'

Roger can be seen as a shadowy character throughout the novel. In this chapter he appears as a sentry, the person responsible for the rock that kills Piggy, and Jack's torturer/executioner.

When we first see him in this chapter, Golding describes Roger's face as 'dark', perhaps reflecting the 'gloomy face' that we saw in Chapter Four. Later in the chapter, we see him at the top of the pinnacles by the rock and the lever that he had so 'admired' in Chapter Ten. The reader knows that up until this point, he has thrown stones 'to miss' at the littluns and Sam and Eric. This time, the onomatopoeic 'Zup!' of Roger's stones dropped on to Ralph and Piggy punctuates the conflict. Roger and the other boys are caught up in the 'incantation of hatred', this word choice suggesting words chanted as a magic spell. This leads Roger 'with a sense of delirious abandonment' to lean on the lever to send the rock towards Ralph and Piggy. This 'abandonment' implies that, caught up in the moment, he sheds any sense of civilisation or humanity.

After Piggy's death, the boys view Roger differently. Golding tells us that the 'hangman's horror', society's distaste towards an executioner, surrounds him. However, Roger accepts this role, leaving his sentry duty as Jack interrogates Sam and Eric. Knowing what Roger is capable of, Golding leaves the reader fearing for their safety at the end of the chapter.

Context

DOIT!

At the end of the chapter, Golding tells us: 'Roger edged past the Chief, only just avoiding pushing him with his shoulder.' What is Golding implying here?

STRETCH IT!

After his experiences in the Second World War, Golding wrote in his collection of essays, *Hot Gates,* published in 1965: 'I believed then, that man was sick — not exceptional man, but average man. I believed that the condition of man was to be a morally diseased creation and that the best job I could do at the time was to trace the connection between his diseased nature and the international mess he gets himself into.'

Write a paragraph to explain how this quotation from Golding is relevant to the events in this chapter.

Chapter Twelve: Cry of the Hunters

Summary

Ralph is hiding and considering his injuries. He decides to head towards Castle Rock. He enters Simon's place in the jungle and, finding the pig's skull on the stick, smashes it. The skull continues to 'grin' at him. Ralph wishes he could just walk into Castle Rock, say 'pax' and pretend they were 'still boys, schoolboys'. The chant *'Kill the beast! Cut his throat! Spill his blood!'* can be heard in the distance.

Seeing two boys, Ralph realises that Sam and Eric are 'part of the tribe' now. He creeps up to them. They tell Ralph that ' – they made us'. Sam and Eric say Ralph is going to be hunted and that Roger has 'sharpened a stick at both ends'. They give him meat. Ralph hears Sam and Eric being punished before sleeping.

Ralph wakes as a savage is searching for him nearby. He evades the hunters, hiding in a 'smashed space' created by the rock that killed Piggy. Ralph hears the twins being tortured by Jack and Roger – they know he will be in the thicket. Jack heaves rocks down on him. He sends down a huge rock and the hunters go into the thicket. They set fire to the thicket and smoke begins to engulf the island.

Ralph tries to think through his escape and runs towards 'the ocean side'. Ralph realises that the island is on fire. The fire is getting closer. Ralph realises the fire will engulf the fruit trees – there will be no food.

A savage's face appears. Ralph screams and runs as the hunters give chase. He falls, seeing one of the shelters burst into flames. He crouches to shield himself, 'trying to cry for mercy'. He looks up and sees a naval officer: rescue! When asked, Ralph says that he is in charge. Ironically, the cruiser saw the smoke from the island's fire. Ralph begins to sob.

DEFINE IT!

antiphonal speech – the twins speak in alternating parts

cordon – a line of police or soldiers

crepitation – crackling, rattling sound

pax – call for a truce used in children's games to avoid being caught

ululation – howling sound

DO IT!

Why does Ralph 'sob' at the end of the novel?

Golding's methods

The final hunt: 'Don't scream. You'll get back.'

All of the features that we have grown accustomed to appear in this hunt, only this time, shockingly, it is a hunt for Ralph. There is the chant, with the subtle change to '*Kill the beast*!' signalling that Ralph is now being framed as the beast in the same way that Simon was the beast 'in disguise', and Roger has a 'stick sharpened at both ends', this time not for a pig but for Ralph.

The final chase is presented as fast, chaotic and out of control. Ralph screams and this is a scream 'of fright and anger and desperation'; this list of emotions linked by 'and' creates a sense of urgency and sets the pace of the hunt. This scream becomes 'continuous' – a primitive cry from his heart. Ralph 'shot forward' – the metaphor linking to gunfire, before he 'burst the thicket' – again relating to the violence of a rupture, before he comes into the open 'screaming, snarling, bloody'. The animal noises reinforce the savage hunt before relentlessly the action continues once again. These jarring noises are muted, as Ralph is 'silent, running'. This pause is momentary as Golding returns to the 'roar' of the forest on fire with a 'great fan-shaped flame'.

Animal imagery

Throughout the final chapter, Golding describes Ralph's behaviour using animal imagery indicating that he too has descended into his most primitive form. The place he sleeps is his 'lair', as he hides from the hunters; he 'found that he had bark in his mouth from the gnawed spear'. Escaping, Ralph finds a 'smallish' savage and with a 'snarling' sound, stabs him. As Golding implies this is one of the littluns, the reader sees how far Ralph has descended from the boy whose 'stillness...marked him out' to the littluns in Chapter One.

Ralph ends up on the beach. Look at the paragraph beginning, 'He stumbled over a root and the cry that pursued him rose even higher.' Write out the paragraph and highlight it to show:

- noise

- sights

- movement

- touch/feeling.

The naval officer

The naval officer arrives, to some extent representing the secure, adult world. The reader, who until this moment has seen Jack as a murderous dictator leading his tribe, suddenly sees Jack through the naval officer's eyes: 'a little boy who wore the remains of an extraordinary black cap on his red hair.' This shift in focus would be funny if it wasn't for the island 'shuddering with flame' like hellfire behind him. The officer continues to misread the situation, thinking it is merely 'fun and games'. He grins 'cheerfully' at Ralph, asking about the boys' 'war': 'Nobody killed, I hope?' He does not expect Ralph's truthful answer, 'Only two.'

DO IT!

Here is a student writing in response to the AQA question: How does Golding present the theme of conflict in *Lord of the Flies*?

Read the student's answer and their teacher's notes alongside.
Develop this answer following the teacher's guidance.

It is interesting that Golding presents this rescue coming from the adult world of warships and military personnel with revolvers and machine guns. The reader sees the parallels between this adult world involved in its own war and the conflicts between the ideals of Ralph and Jack on the island.

You need to link your ideas to the theme of conflict. Add to this paragraph to make this link. You might want to add Golding's use of irony here. Support your ideas with **evidence** from the novel. To target AO1, return to your quotation and pick out specific words from the quotation to analyse.

 STRETCH IT!

Do you think the ending of *Lord of the Flies* is satisfying? Explain your ideas.

Character and theme essentials

Golding's methods

Civilisation versus savagery: 'a stick sharpened at both ends'

Sam and Eric tell Ralph that Roger has 'sharpened a stick at both ends'. Ralph cannot comprehend what this might mean. But the reader knows the implications. It will be Ralph's head that goes on to the stick as an offering to the beast. The reader then begins to wonder what will happen to the rest of Ralph's body. After the hunt there will be a feast. Is Golding suggesting here that the boys will break down the final taboo of feasting on human flesh?

DO IT!

Golding presents the 'trim cruiser' as the final image in the novel. How does this image link to Golding's message?

Golding's message: 'end of innocence'

As Roger and Jack descend into torture and murder, we also see Ralph animal-like in his own savagery for self-defence. The naval officer sees the 'tiny tots' with the 'distended bellies of small savages' and thinks that 'British boys…would have been able to put up a better show than that.' Replying that 'it had been like that at first', Ralph weeps, with the narrator taking over to voice Golding's message, for 'the end of innocence, the darkness of a man's heart'.

Character development

Roger: 'He's a terror'

It is in these final four chapters that the darkness at the heart of Roger's nature surfaces. In Chapter Four, when throwing stones at Henry, 'he aimed to miss'; by Chapter Eleven, he is dropping stones on Ralph and Piggy before, with 'delirious abandonment', levering the rock that kills Piggy. This 'abandonment' releases Roger from any 'taboo of the old life' as he assumes the 'hangman's horror' in the eyes of the tribe and begins to wield his 'nameless authority'.

Symbolism

The death of Piggy: 'the true, wise friend called Piggy'

When Piggy – the voice of reason – dies, the boys' descent into savagery speeds up, with even Ralph succumbing to savage acts in his fight for survival. When faced with the 'cry of the hunters', Ralph cannot think through what would be the most 'sensible thing to do' for there is 'no Piggy to talk sense'. It is fitting that the conch, the symbol of order, should be shattered as Piggy dies. A rational society needs 'rules' and order to shape it. In Ralph's society, the conch provides this. In Jack's autocratic society, order is maintained by fear and punishment.

REVIEW IT!

1 What does Simon find on the top of the mountain?

2 When Ralph and Piggy go to Castle Rock in Chapter Nine, how is Jack presented?

3 When Ralph tries to assert his leadership by saying that he has the conch, what does Jack say?

4 Piggy advises that he and Ralph should leave as a storm begins to brew; what reason does he give?

5 How does Ralph behave in the dance?

6 When Ralph says, 'That was murder' about Simon, how does Piggy respond?

7 Where do Sam and Eric claim to have been during the dance?

8 Why does Jack beat Wilfred?

9 What does Jack steal from Ralph's shelter?

10 What does Piggy initially fear Jack and his hunters had come to steal?

11 When Ralph and Piggy go to Castle Rock in Chapter Eleven, where is Jack?

12 The pig is 'headless'. Why is this important?

13 What does Ralph call Jack?

14 Who levers the rock on to Piggy?

15 What happens to Piggy's body?

16 What injuries does Ralph receive when he fights Jack?

17 What does Ralph find in Simon's special place and what does he do to it?

18 Who are last to join Jack's tribe?

19 How does the naval officer describe the littluns?

20 Why do you think Golding begins and ends the novel on the beach?

Characters

Ralph (the protagonist)

What do we know about Ralph?

- Ralph is the first character that we meet on the island. He is 'The boy with fair hair' – the opening line.

- Ralph is elected chief.

- Ralph and Jack are engaged in a power struggle throughout the novel.

- Ralph works to create a civilised society with order, shelter and rescue.

- Ralph also begins to descend into savagery as the novel progresses, especially after Piggy's death.

- By the end of the novel he is alone, being chased by Jack and his tribe in a deadly hunt.

- He steps forward as the leader at the end of the novel in response to the naval officer.

How Golding presents Ralph

How does he behave?

- Ralph's focus is on rescue and shelter.

- He protects Piggy against Jack and develops respect for Piggy's intelligence and wisdom.

- He is brave when he goes to confront the beast on the top of the mountain.

- Ralph yearns for home and the safety of his previous life. He hates the dirt of his clothes and his need of a haircut.

- Ralph discovers the thrill of hunting and gets caught up in the frenzy of the dance that ends with Simon's death. He stabs a 'smallish' savage as he tries to escape the hunt at the end of the novel.

How is he described?

- Physically, 'he might make a boxer...but there was a mildness about his mouth and eyes that proclaimed no devil.'

- Ralph is 12 years old with blond hair.

What does he represent?

- Ralph represents democracy and morality – doing the right thing.

- He can represent the force of good in the struggle between good and evil.

NAIL IT!

The character of Ralph is useful when writing about all of the themes but is key to the themes of savagery, civilisation and the end of innocence as he contrasts with Jack.

Ralph's leadership

- Ralph's leadership centres on looking after the group, in this case establishing shelter, a clean place to live and fire for rescue.

- Unlike Jack, Ralph does not seek personal power.

- He works with Piggy as his advisor representing reason and intelligence.

Here are two students writing an answer to the AQA exam question: How does Golding present Ralph's leadership in *Lord of the Flies*?

Student answer A

Golding presents Ralph as the embodiment of democracy in the novel. He represents the theme of civilisation where an ideal society ensures that each person has a voice that is listened to. His first act as 'Chief' on the island is to establish the assembly (a democratic parliament) and the rule of the conch allowing the person holding it the right to speak and be heard. It is no accident that one of the first people to speak in the second assembly is one of the littluns. They represent the common people, and through the conch, Ralph's form of leadership allows them a voice. However, when the littlun introduces the 'snake-thing', Ralph meets the beast's existence or not with rational argument, contrasting with Jack's rash declaration that his hunters will 'kill it'.

Student answer B

Golding presents Ralph as the embodiment of democracy in the novel; however, Ralph's form of government is shown to break down in the face of the 'darkness of man's heart'. As the novel progresses, we see Ralph struggling with thinking through his ideas as if a 'shutter had come down'. When Ralph's sensible leadership confronts the thrill of Jack's violence and hunting, he cannot win. Through his democratic leadership, Ralph is unable to get the boys to obey the rule of bringing fresh water. In Jack's camp, through his autocratic rule Jack's orders are obeyed and 'coco-nut shells' are 'full of drink'.

DO IT!

1 Decide which student – A or B – expresses a view that is closest to yours. Perhaps you agree with both students.

2 Write a paragraph explaining your own response to the question: How does Golding present Ralph's leadership?

Evidence

You might not agree with what one or both these students say about Ralph, but notice how they use evidence to support their thoughts. They use two sorts of evidence: they refer to parts of the novel, and they quote relevant words. Both of the students build quotations naturally into their own sentences.

 STRETCH IT!

At the end of the novel, Ralph understands and weeps for the 'darkness of man's heart'. How do you think Ralph will adjust to real life, away from the island?

Jack (the antagonist)

What do we know about Jack?

- Jack is the leader of the choir before becoming the leader of the hunters.

- Jack thinks he should be chief but loses the vote to Ralph.

- Jack becomes obsessed with hunting, leading him to paint his face and develop primitive rituals of chanting, dancing, a re-enactment after the kill.

- He splits from Ralph and leads his own tribe at Castle Rock.

- Under his leadership, both Simon and Piggy die and he leads the hunt for Ralph, presumably to kill him.

- As leader, he beats Wilfred for an unknown crime and tortures the twins.

NAILIT!

It is important when writing about the novel that you show how the characters develop Golding's themes and message of the novel. The character of Jack is useful when writing about all of the themes, but he is key to the themes of savagery, civilisation and the end of innocence as he contrasts with Ralph.

How Golding presents Jack

How is he described?

- Jack is tall and thin with red hair.

- Jack's face is 'ugly without silliness'.

- His blue eyes are 'ready to turn to anger'.

What does he represent?

Jack represents autocratic leadership and amorality – not caring about right or wrong.

Jack can represent the force of evil in the struggle between good and evil.

Jack's leadership

Jack can be seen as a natural leader. As leader of the choir, his autocratic style of leadership is shown from the first chapter. The choir march in formation along the beach, 'Wearily obedient' in the heat, and Ralph notes immediately that 'This was the voice of one who knew his own mind.' When Jack splits from Ralph, he no longer has to respect the rules of civilisation and he becomes an autocratic leader demanding obedience and adulation. He presents himself 'garlanded' as a god-like figure, and he controls the tribe through his manipulation of their fear of the beast, beatings and torture. He becomes 'a terror'. It is no accident that whereas Ralph's alliance is with Piggy, the voice of intelligence, Jack's alliance is with Roger, the executioner.

The kills

Jack's descent into savagery can be seen through the growing violence of the kills in the novel. The first time he encounters a pig, Jack is unable to kill it. Humiliated by this perceived weakness he then goes on to kill. From here, killing for the thrill of 'imposing' his 'will' is more important than killing for survival and meat. Simon's death under his leadership as a result of 'our dance' could be seen as an example of the group's loss of control. However, his response to Piggy's death is to scream at Ralph 'wildly', 'See? See? That's what you'll get!' suggesting that all sense of morality has been lost and murder is not taboo in his world. Indeed, at the end of the novel we see Jack leading a hunt for Ralph with a 'stick sharpened at both ends' presumably for Ralph's head as an offering to the beast.

Jack's conflict with Piggy

Jack's conflict with Piggy starts from their first meeting when Jack dismisses him with the brutal, 'You're talking too much…Shut up, Fatty.' Piggy represents intelligence and reason: he is seen thinking scientifically; he thinks about how to create clocks on the island, for example. Under a dictator, there is no tolerance of people who may question the dictator's decisions or speak out against them: 'We know who ought to say things.' In far-right regimes there is often mistrust of science and academic thought – something Golding saw under Hitler's leadership of Germany in the Second World War. Jack's form of autocratic leadership will not tolerate Piggy, who questions, 'Which is better – to have rules and agree, or to hunt and kill?'

DO IT!

Find three quotations about Jack.

- Underline key methods.
- Summarise Jack's symbolic significance.

STRETCH IT!

Some critics argue that Jack is a much more interesting character than Ralph. How far do you agree?

Simon

What do we know about Simon?

- The first time we meet Simon he faints and we learn that this often happens to him.

- He helps others: he shares his meat with Piggy and he helps the littluns reach fruit.

- Simon accompanies Ralph and Jack on the first expedition.

- He tries to help Ralph with the shelters.

- Simon predicts that Ralph will get home.

- Simon hallucinates as he talks with the pig's head on a stick.

- Simon is unafraid of the jungle and happily goes into the jungle alone.

- Simon bravely goes to see if the beast is on top of the mountain.

- As he tries to tell his truth of the dead airman, he is killed. The boys believe, in their frenzy, that he is the beast.

- His body is washed out to sea.

How Golding presents Simon

How is he described?

- Simon is described as a 'skinny, vivid little boy with a glance coming up from under a hut of straight hair that hung down, black and coarse'.

- He doesn't believe in the beast as reported by Sam and Eric: 'Simon, walking in front of Ralph, felt a flicker of incredulity – a beast with claws that scratched, that sat on a mountain-top, that left no tracks and yet was not fast enough to catch Samneric.'

- Simon understands 'the picture of a human, at once heroic and sick' that it is 'part of you'.

What does he represent?

Simon represents goodness and kindness as well as the force of spiritual goodness. He can be seen to represent a Christ-figure on the island. He 'suffers the little children' and finally dies in his attempt to bring the truth to the boys.

NAILIT!

The character of Simon is useful when writing about all of the themes, but he is key to the themes of savagery, civilisation and the end of innocence. When writing about the theme of good versus evil, Simon represents spiritual good.

DOIT!

Find three quotations about Simon.

- Underline key methods.

- Summarise Simon's symbolic significance.

Piggy

What do we know about Piggy?

- Piggy is the second character we meet on the island; his reaction to the fruit, 'them fruit', means that his introduction is undignified.

- Piggy tells Ralph how to use the conch.

- He confides his nickname to Ralph and is betrayed when Ralph relays this to the other boys.

- Piggy is intelligent.

- Piggy has medical problems such as 'ass-mar'. He is also overweight, from a lower class than the other boys and needs glasses – all factors that set him apart from the rest.

- He is bullied and dismissed by Jack.

- He is murdered by Roger.

- We do not learn his real name.

How Golding presents Piggy

How is he described?

- Piggy is 'shorter' than Ralph and 'very fat'.

- Piggy refers to 'grown-ups' frequently and can be viewed as adult-like in his opinions. This reference to the adult world shows his reliance on society's expectations and makes him different from the other boys.

- Piggy understands that the beast isn't real – his intelligence and scientific knowledge do not allow this belief.

- Ralph's ideas either come from Piggy or are supported by his thinking, for example, use of the conch and the focus on rescue.

- Piggy lacks Ralph's charisma or Jack's authority to lead the boys, despite their understanding that 'what intelligence had been shown was traceable to Piggy'.

What does he represent?

Piggy represents the voice of reason and intelligence. His glasses enable him to see the world clearly, but his lack of Ralph or Jack's charisma means that the boys will not recognise his ideas. Once Piggy dies, taking with him the conch, all reason and order dies on the island too, leaving Jack's savagery in control.

It is interesting that Piggy's glasses, representing scientific reasoning and clear sight, become the most valuable object on the island. There can be no rescue, security or meat without them. They become more valuable to the boys than the conch, the symbol of order.

NAILIT!

The character of Piggy is useful when writing about all of the themes but he is key to the themes of savagery, civilisation and the end of innocence.

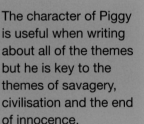

DOIT!

Find three quotations about Piggy.

- Underline key methods.

- Summarise Piggy's symbolic significance.

Sam and Eric (Samneric)

What do we know about Sam and Eric?

- Sam and Eric are identical twins.

- The boys are always together and become known by one name, Samneric.

- They are part of the 'biguns'.

- They see the dead airman and imagine that it is the beast. In their fear, they believe it follows them.

- Originally part of the choir, they remain with Ralph when Jack leaves.

- They are captured and tortured by Jack and Roger.

- They are forced to join Jack's tribe.

- Under pressure, they reveal Ralph's hiding place in the final chapter.

NAILIT!

When you are writing about characters, it is important to remember that Golding purposely creates each character. They are not real people. You may find it helpful to use 'Golding presents...' when you write about characters.

How Golding presents Sam and Eric

How are they described?

- They share 'identical laughter'.

- They finish each other's sentences ('antiphonal speech').

- 'They could never manage to do things sensibly if that meant acting independently.'

- In Chapter One, they are presented 'panting at Ralph like dogs'. This image suggests their loyalty to Ralph, which will remain until the end of the novel.

What do they represent?

Sam and Eric represent followers rather than leaders – ordinary people, like all of us. They tell Jack and Roger where Ralph is hiding, a Biblical **allusion** to Judas's betrayal of Christ.

Roger

What do we know about Roger?

- Roger is a member of the choir and one of the hunters.
- Roger suggests having a vote for chief in Chapter One.
- During the killing of the sow he pushes the stick into the sow's anus – revealing his savagery.
- At first, he doesn't throw stones at Henry because of the 'taboo of the old life'.
- Roger joins Ralph and Jack on the 'mad expedition' to find the beast in Chapter Seven.
- Roger drops stones down on to Ralph and Piggy.
- Roger levers the rock on to Piggy, killing him.
- He tortures Sam and Eric.
- Sam and Eric tell Ralph that the following day, 'The Chief and Roger' are 'going to do you'.

How Golding presents Roger

How is he described?

- Roger is a 'slight' and 'furtive boy', 'uncommunicative by nature'.
- When Jack calls him away from watching the littluns, 'a darker shadow crept beneath the swarthiness of his skin'.
- He has 'no opinion on the beast'.
- When challenged by the sentries at Castle Rock he states, 'You couldn't stop me coming if I wanted.'
- When told about Wilfred being tied up waiting to be beaten, he sits, 'assimilating the possibilities of irresponsible authority' instead of trying to stop it.
- After Piggy's death, he attains an aura of 'The hangman's horror' in the eyes of the others.
- When 'edging past' Jack in Chapter Eleven, he only just avoids 'pushing him with his shoulder'.
- He wields a 'nameless authority'.

What does he represent?

Roger represents pure evil and brutality. Roger enjoys torturing and killing people as an end in itself (unlike Jack, who becomes brutal in his quest for power and leadership).

At the end of Chapter Eleven, Golding suggests that Roger will ultimately challenge Jack for power, as he only just avoids 'pushing him with his shoulder', which is a chilling thought for the reader.

Littluns

What do we know about them?

- The littluns are a group of small children around six years of age.

- They spend their days playing together and tend to keep out of the politics of the group.

- Although Ralph cares for their welfare, they are largely ignored by Jack and his hunters, other than Jack's quip about killing one in their re-enactment of the hunt.

- Ralph and Piggy do not manage to work out how many of them there are.

- The boy with the mulberry-coloured birthmark first mentions the beast, the 'snake-thing'. It is likely that he is killed in the first fire.

How Golding presents the littluns

How are they described?

- At the end of the novel they are described by the naval officer as 'tiny tots' with their 'distended bellies of small savages'.

- Ralph describes the littluns as talking and screaming at night as if 'it wasn't a good island'. Jack replies, 'They're batty.'

What do they represent?

The littluns represent the common people, the general public who get on with their lives unaffected by the power struggles around them. They also represent the end of innocence, as they cry at night and are tormented by Roger and Maurice.

Percival Wemys Madison particularly represents the end of innocence. At the start of the novel he can recite his address; however, by the end of the novel this 'incantation' has 'faded clean away'.

DO IT!

How does Golding present the naval officer?

• What do we know about the naval officer? (What does he do within the **plot**?)

• How is the naval officer described? (What does he look like and how does he behave?)

• What does the naval officer represent?

REVIEW

IT!

1 How old are Ralph and Jack at the start of the novel?

2 Who tries to make a list of names at the start of the novel?

3 'Ralph's leadership is about leading people rather than a quest for power.' Is this true or false?

4 What object enables Ralph to become chief?

5 Who is described as being 'ugly without silliness'?

6 Who suggests that the boys should vote for a chief?

7 When Jack says that he should be chief, what qualities does he list?

8 What does Piggy represent?

9 What Biblical figure could Simon represent?

10 What theme is exemplified through the character of Percival?

11 How does Jack behave after Piggy dies?

12 What message is Simon bringing to the boys when he is killed?

13 Which character recites his name and address as an incantation?

14 In Chapter Ten, Sam and Eric begin fighting each other. We are not told why. Why does Golding include this detail?

15 Who meets Sam and Eric's tale of being chased by the beast with 'incredulity'?

16 What prophecy does Simon make about Ralph?

17 Which two boys destroy the littluns' sandcastles?

18 Who incites terror in Sam and Eric?

19 How does the naval officer view the boys? Explain your ideas.

20 Which character has developed the most by the end of the novel? Explain your ideas.

Themes and contexts

Savagery versus civilisation

Rules: 'the rules are the only thing we've got!'

When the boys first arrive on the island, under Ralph's leadership they begin to set up a civilisation that is similar to the society they had come from and the society that both a post-war reader as well as a modern reader would recognise. This society has assemblies, where voting is used to make democratic decisions, replicating the structure of Parliament. Ralph's society also has 'rules' – just like our laws – to ensure that society works in an orderly way for all. Jack's initial response to rules is seemingly positive, 'We'll have rules!...Lots of rules! Then if anyone breaks 'em – I.' Despite Jack embracing the idea of rules, his focus on punishment for anyone breaking the rules is clear. Later in the novel, we see Wilfred tied up waiting to be beaten for some misbehaviour that is not clear to Sam and Eric or the reader. Here we see Jack's approach to the rules. When those rules don't suit his purposes ('The conch doesn't count on top of the mountain') he will shed them, but he maintains his focus on punishment as a means of controlling the tribe.

Brutality: 'He was batty. He asked for it.'

In the novel we see many acts of brutality that increase in their severity as the novel progresses. This fits with Golding's message of the darkness within all humankind. However, within autocratic leadership absolute power can also lead to acts of brutality (see also page 71).

(see also page 71)

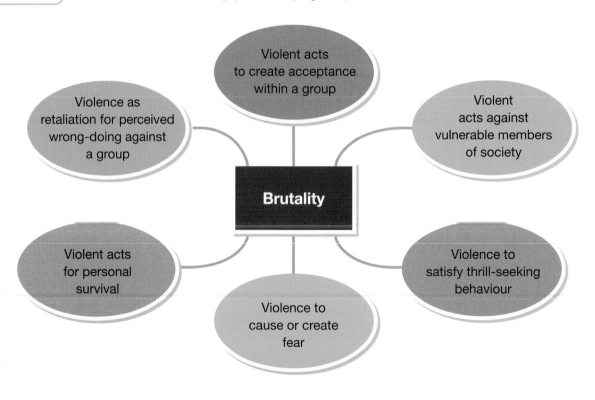

- Violent acts to create acceptance within a group
- Violence as retaliation for perceived wrong-doing against a group
- Violent acts against vulnerable members of society
- **Brutality**
- Violent acts for personal survival
- Violence to satisfy thrill-seeking behaviour
- Violence to cause or create fear

DO IT!

1 For each type of brutality, annotate with a character from the novel, specific events and what it shows you about Golding's message.

2 Using your annotations in the diagram, are any examples more acceptable than others? Explain your ideas.

Painted faces: 'The mask compelled them.'

Jack is able to shield himself from his actions through the use of face paints to create a mask. It is the thought of this mask that terrifies Sam and Eric and 'compels' the hunters to obey him. As with many things on the island, the intention begins fairly innocently. Jack wants to camouflage himself as he hunts the pigs, 'Like in the war.' However, once he has painted his face 'an awesome stranger' astonishes him. This transformation liberates him 'from shame and self-consciousness' enabling him to commit acts that up until this point he had hesitated to do. By Chapter Nine, Jack is Chief of his own tribe and wears the mask to represent his power. By Chapter Eleven, the other boys are also 'freed by the paint', before becoming completely unrecognisable in Chapter Twelve. Here, Ralph sees someone 'striped brown, black and red'. Ralph thinks it may be Bill, but 'this was not Bill. This was a savage whose image refused to blend with that ancient picture of a boy in shorts and shirt.'

Rituals: 'Do our dance!'

The dance begins as an expression of the excitement of the hunt. This takes a sinister turn as it becomes 'our' dance. The possessive pronoun indicates that this now belongs to the hunters. The dance gives the hunters a sense of belonging to the group, effectively establishing the group's separate identity. The dance develops further as the boys take on the role of the pig. This is taken a step further when the dance becomes so out of control that Robert is hurt. In the final chapter, it is Ralph who is being hunted and the reader can only speculate whether one of the littluns will be used to represent the 'pig' when Ralph's head is on the stick.

Clothes: 'except for a pair of tattered shorts...he was naked'

One of the ways that Golding presents the boy's descent into savagery is through their clothes. As they shed their clothes, they shed their civilisation.

DO IT!

1 Find three quotations to show how Jack's clothing changes throughout the novel.

2 Throughout the novel, Ralph is concerned about the length of his hair and his dirty clothing. Why does Golding add this detail?

STRETCH IT!

Why do you think Piggy refuses to face up to his part in the violence connected to Simon's death?

End of innocence

The 18th-century philosopher Jean-Jacques Rousseau influenced the concept of childhood innocence. He believed that children are born good and sin-free; it is only through life experiences that they learn to do evil things. Through his experience as a teacher however, Golding witnessed children behaving brutally towards each other. This view of childhood is explored in the novel.

When the boys arrive on the island, it is established as a 'good island' with access to food and water. It is also free of adults and their rules and restrictions. Although the boys establish their rules, it becomes pretty clear that they are unable to stick to them. As Ralph complains in Chapter Three, 'They're hopeless…They're off bathing, or eating, or playing' instead of sticking to the agreement of building the shelters. It is also Jack, of course, who declares, 'Bollocks to the rules!' Golding's use of the swear word here also shows that taboos are beginning to break down as well as order and rules.

It is only Piggy who questions the boys' behaviour, drawing attention to how it would be seen through an adult's eyes: 'What's grown-ups goin' to think?' However, Piggy's lack of status in the boys' eyes results in his questions 'What are we? Humans? Or animals? Or savages?' being ignored.

Simon's death through the participation of the boys in the frenzied dance shows the evil within them all. It is this loss that causes Ralph to sob on the beach at the end of the novel as he weeps for 'the end of innocence, the darkness of a man's heart'.

Percival Wemys Madison

Percival has obviously been taught his name and address by his parents in case he is ever lost. Golding shows the end of his innocence through his memory breaking down until, at the end, the 'incantation had faded clean away'. Percival is lost on the island, but the 'incantation', the magical spell, has not worked. The knowledge that civilisation can't help him leads him to hide in a shelter 'for two days, talking, singing and crying'.

DO IT!

In the last chapter, where Ralph is chased by the hunters, Ralph stabs a 'smallish' savage. Explain how this episode fits into the theme of the end of innocence.

STRETCH IT!

How does Golding show Simon's loss of innocence?

Power

Political power: Jack

Jack pursues political power for the love of power itself. Jack rules the boys through fear. He manipulates their fear of the beast and becomes himself an object of fear. This shows us how rulers can use the power of superstition and religion to control people.

Gaining power over others: Roger

Through Roger we see the power humans enjoy wielding over others. We see him throwing stones at the littluns as they are playing and we see him destroying their sandcastles – seemingly the enjoyment of bullying. However, this enjoyment develops in the final chapters as we see him surrounded by the 'nameless authority' of the executioner.

The power of fear: the beast

Golding presents fear as something inside all of us. We aren't taught to be scared; instead we find things to be scared of. Fear of the beast controls the boys' behaviour. They will not enter the forest alone at night. The littluns cry and scream at night.

Power

The power of the mob: killing the pig

When the hunters kill the sow they are described as 'racing, fierce, wedded in lust, laughing'. The scene reveals the power of the mob as the boys chase the pig down and slowly stab a spear 'inch by inch' into the animal, causing a 'high-pitched scream'. It is also the power of the mob that results in Simon's death.

The power of the natural world

Golding presents the island as a place of powerful beauty. However, there is a darker side to the natural world, where once again Golding explores the two sides of power. In this case, the natural world can be seen through the dual nature of fire as a source of comfort and a powerful destroyer. We see the fruit as a powerful source of food as well as a source of diahorrea and stomach cramps. The power of the sea to claim the bodies of the airman, Simon and Piggy is also shown.

DO IT!

We are told about Jack that, 'Authority sat on his shoulder and chattered in his ear like an ape.' Explain Golding's methods in this quotation.

DEFINE IT!

democracy – a system of government where people vote to support elected representatives

autocracy – a system of government where one ruler holds power; this person has supreme power

Politics

Golding's political message: styles of leadership

Ralph and Jack can be viewed as representing opposite political ideas. This leads to conflict between them.

Within a democracy: Ralph

> The small boy held out his hands for the conch

✓ Everyone has a voice and equal power.

> 'Seems to me we ought to have a chief to decide things.'
>
> 'A chief! A chief!'

✓ If a society is split on an issue, it can help to heal rifts because decisions are seen as being the majority **viewpoint** with everyone having the opportunity to air their view.

> This toy of voting was almost as pleasing as the conch.

✓ It encourages personal involvement. People control their own outcomes.

After Jack asserts himself as being the best choice for chief:

> The dark boy, Roger, stirred at last and spoke up.
>
> 'Let's have a vote.'

✓ It stops exploitation and corruption.

✗ It focuses solely on the needs and desires of the majority – so can create a 'them versus us' way of thinking.

✗ A person who has an expert opinion has as much power as someone with no general knowledge.

✗ Making decisions can be time consuming. An emergency situation would need to be voted on, slowing down the rate of response.

Within an autocracy: Jack

> I ought to be chief…because I'm chapter chorister and head boy.

✓ The leader is the voice of authority in all things.

> He's going to beat Wilfred… I don't know he didn't say.

✓ The leader holds absolute power.

> 'To-morrow,' went on the Chief, 'we shall hunt again.'

✓ There will be no opposition, so decisions and plans can be made and followed through quickly.

> He's a proper Chief, isn't he?

✓ If people have faith in their leader, it can bring a sense of security as they will see their leader acting for the good of the group.

✗ Power is only wielded by one person, which can lead to corruption.

✗ No elections will mean that the ruler can stay in power indefinitely.

✗ If rules are not followed, brutal punishments can follow with no checks.

Golding's viewpoint: autocracy

Golding was outspoken about autocracy and how it can take over a country without people noticing. He had witnessed the impact of this leadership through the rise of Nazi Germany, which led to the Second World War. In his collection of essays, *Hot Gates*, published in 1965, he wrote: 'My book was to say you think that now the war is over and an evil thing destroyed, you are safe because you are naturally kind and decent. But I know why the thing rose in Germany. I know it could happen in any country. It could happen here.'

Golding states that even though we may consider ourselves kind and decent – like Ralph – the rise of right-wing autocracy could happen to our country, it is not necessarily just confined to Germany. He shows this possibility in the novel through Ralph's discovery of the thrill of hunting and his participation in the frenzy leading to Simon's death. Through these scenes he is showing the reader that no one is exempt. Even Piggy – the voice of reason – participates, as do Sam and Eric. Good, loyal and decent people can get caught up too. It is not just the territory of those who seek power.

DO IT!

At the start of the novel, the boys realise that the intelligent ideas come from Piggy. Why don't the boys suggest that he is chief rather than Ralph?

STRETCH IT!

Piggy is part of a democratic way of thinking. In a government, what role do you think he could represent?

Context

Context means one or all of the following:

- ideas and influences at the time the novel was written
- ideas and expectations a modern reader might bring to the novel
- how a scene or episode in a chapter fits into the whole novel.

Using contextual information

Here are parts of two different students' exam answers. The references to context are shown underlined:

Student answer A

Within the theme of savagery that dominates the novel, Golding explores the violence that the boys inflict on each other as well as on the pigs on the island. This savagery, shown to be 'part of you', <u>reflects the brutality he saw during the Second World War. The events in the novel may seen dramatic to us now, but readers in 1954, having seen the rise of the Nazi Party, would have understood why Golding chose to show how people will seek to gain power over others, especially autocratic leaders,</u> like Jack.

Student answer B

<u>William Golding was born in Cornwall in the UK in 1911. He started teaching English and philosophy in Salisbury. In 1940 he joined the Royal Navy. Lord of the Flies was his first novel and was published in 1954 but was written in 1953.</u>

NAIL IT!

By all means, allow what you know of the novel's context to help you to write meaningfully about the key element given to you in your exam question. However, in general, the best rule is to let the novel speak for itself: don't read too much into it by trying to make it explain aspects of Golding's life. Focus on your reaction to the novel and the methods Golding has used to create that reaction in you.

Answer B will probably make you think, 'and your point is?' The contextual information given might be correct, but it is not helpful. In fact, it is all context and no comment. By contrast, the contextual information in answer A *adds* to our understanding of the novel by shedding light on the significance of a key idea in the novel.

A typical AQA exam-style question where context could be used might be:

AQA exam-style question

How does Golding use the boys on the island to explore ideas about childhood?

'ideas about childhood' is a clear focus for the question. Golding's presentation of childhood is a matter of *your thoughtful opinion*. You *might* assess Golding's presentation of childhood partly in the context of:

- the typical presentation of childhood at the time the novel was written, for example, *The Coral Island, The Famous Five* series
- what you think about childhood.

The Second World War's impact on Golding's thinking

In his collection of essays, *Hot Gates*, written in 1965, Golding outlines how the brutality within the Second World War changed his view of society and the good within humankind: 'The overall intention may be stated simply enough. Before the Second World War, I believed in the perfectibility of social man; that a correct structure of society would produce goodwill; and that therefore you could remove all social ills by a reorganisation of society...but after the war I did not because I was unable to.'

When discussing the atrocities that happened during the war, Golding states: 'They were not done by the headhunters of New Guinea or by some primitive tribe in the Amazon. They were done, skillfully, coldly, by educated men, doctors, lawyers, by men with a tradition of civilization behind them, to beings of their own kind.'

The nuclear threat

Golding uses Piggy to tell the reader that the boys are on the island because they are escaping an atomic bomb. When Golding was writing the novel, the threat of nuclear war was very real, especially as it followed the use of an atomic bomb on Hiroshima in 1945 that brought the war to an end. This threat, plus the horrors of the holocaust, are reflected in the themes of the novel.

NAILIT!

AQA points out that the best way to write usefully about context is:

- to make sure you answer the question
- to only include contextual information that supports a point you are making.

DOIT!

Why do you think Golding uses an atomic bomb as the reason why the boys are on the island?

Golding's social message: 'man produces evil as a bee produces honey'

The novel can be described as an allegory for the wider social ills Golding saw not only during the post-war period when the novel was written, but also during the Second World War (see page 73). In *Lord of the Flies*, Golding shows the reader that all humankind will descend to savagery and evil if not checked by society's rules.

In Chapter Five, when the boys are discussing the beast, Simon tries to articulate his understanding of the beast: 'maybe it's only us'. The boys dismiss this, but Golding returns to it in Chapter Eight. Here, Jack has left a gift for the beast. Unbeknown to him, he has placed this gift of a pig's head on a stick in Simon's sanctuary. The head on the stick has become 'Lord of the Flies', literally translating as Beelzebub, or Satan.

Coming out of his fit, Simon begins a conversation with the Lord of the Flies. He tells him the central message of the novel: 'You knew didn't you? I'm part of you...I'm the reason it's no go? Why things are what they are?'

Golding presents the evils in society as being caused by failings in human nature (a lust for power, savagery, destruction). It is the evils within humankind that will make everything a 'no go' – not work. Without rules to guide us, humankind will always give in to these failings and descend to savagery.

DO IT!

If the pig's head represents the beast, what could the flies that swarm over the 'obscene thing' that 'grinned and dripped' represent?

REVIEW  IT!

1 Which one of the following is the best definition of 'theme'?
   a something the novel is about
   b the language choices made by the writer
   c the order in which things happen in the novel

2 Give three other words that mean (or roughly mean) savagery.

3 Give three other words that mean (or roughly mean) power.

4 Give three other words that mean (or roughly mean) civilisation.

5 Give three other words that mean (or roughly mean) conflict.

6 Name three objects that Jack uses to show his power as chief.

7 Golding served in the Royal Navy during the Second World War. Why is this important?

8 The boys are fleeing from an atom bomb. How does this link to the context of the novel?

9 What does the pig's head on a stick represent?

10 What one word sums up Ralph's form of leadership?

11 What one word sums up Jack's form of leadership?

12 Name three different forms of power that we see in the novel.

13 What theme does Percival Wemys Madison represent?

14 What do clothes represent in the novel?

15 What form of government uses voting as a decision-making process?

16 How does Golding show the reader that the conflict in the adult world is continuing while the boys are on the island?

17 Is the novel's message still relevant today?

18 Explain why 'our dance' is important to the hunters.

19 When Jack paints his face, an 'awesome stranger' confronts him. Explain why this is important.

20 Explain how Golding's presentation of childhood is different from other literature and thinking at the time of the publication of *Lord of the Flies*.

Language, structure and form

Language

How Golding uses language to increase tension

When we talk about the language of a text, we mean how the writer *chooses* words to create effects. In other words, we are studying the writer's word *choices*.

In Chapter Twelve, we see Ralph being chased by Jack's hunters. Towards the end of the chase, Golding uses language to manipulate the reader's emotions as we see the action through Ralph's eyes. (Ralph is hiding in bushes.)

DO IT!

Find a further extract from Chapter Twelve. Analyse it to show the methods Golding uses to increase tension.

Example from the text	How this language is used by Golding
"He laid his cheek against the chocolate-coloured earth,"	This is a comforting image with associations of childhood with the softness of a baby's 'cheek' and the sweetness of 'chocolate'. However, this is a chase to the death and Ralph is fighting a very adult war.
"or perhaps there was a sound"	We are seeing the action through Ralph's eyes. Golding uses tentative language 'or perhaps' to show Ralph's wandering thoughts. In this section of the book, Golding connects a series of clauses to offer different alternatives to the noises that surround Ralph.
"Someone cried out."	The short sentence dramatically wrenches Ralph and the reader out of circling thoughts.
"Hide, break the line, climb a tree – which was best after all?"	Golding signals the urgency of Ralph's thoughts now. This list of imperative verbs 'Hide...break...climb' shows Ralph commanding himself to act. This call to action is broken by the dash as Ralph's indecision takes over, shown by the final question.
"Now the fire was nearer; those volleying shots were great limbs, trunks even, bursting. The fools!"	Again, Golding uses a series of clauses to show Ralph's thoughts. Notice the naturalistic speech of 'trunks even' to show Ralph's inner monologue, as if he is adding a detail as an afterthought. A gun and war metaphor 'volleying shots' brings the reader back to the deadly war between Jack and Ralph. Here is a violent image again 'bursting', relating to the guns and what happens in the frenzy of war. The exclamation 'The fools!' – an adult-sounding statement – breaks the chain of thought.
"Ralph stirred restlessly in his narrow bed."	Golding returns to a childhood image suggesting the comfort and security of home. This juxtaposes with the seriousness of Ralph's situation.

Golding's use of contrasts: beauty and horror

Golding uses layers of description to build a sense of the island as both a place of beauty and a place of potential horror. When Ralph first goes to Castle Rock, he 'shuddered'. Golding then begins to show the reader why Ralph senses this atmosphere.

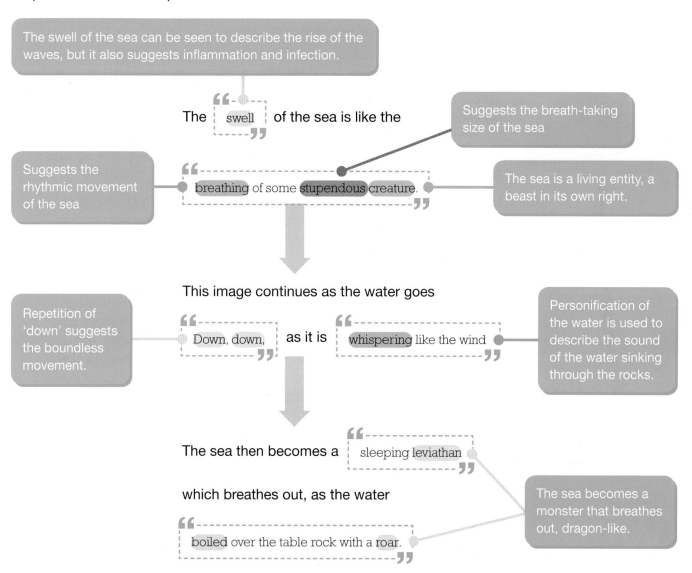

The beauty of the sea is shown in these animal images. However, as Golding develops these images, they take on a sinister edge.

We see this again when we see Simon in his place of sanctuary with the 'dripping' and grinning pig's head. Here the gore of the 'spilled guts' contrasts with the beauty of the descriptions of the clouds as towers, 'grey and cream and copper-coloured'. However, these clouds are 'bulging' suggesting they are distended and swollen, linking back to the fly-covered guts.

These layers of details to create layers of meaning can be seen in the description of the naval officer. The officer's uniform is described to show its precision and its cleanliness, in contrast to the 'filthy' boys. However, the 'revolver' reminds the reader that the officer is dressed for battle in the same way that Jack and his hunters, with 'sticks in their hands', are dressed for their battle.

Throughout the novel Golding uses schoolboy slang, swearing and crude language. Why does he include this language?

Character and language

When you consider the characters, notice the language choices used by Golding to present them. For example, once Jack leaves Ralph's side of the island, he assumes the name of 'Chief', which soon develops to 'The Chief.' In Chapter One, Jack is scathing of 'kids' names', wanting to be called Merridew. However, by the end of the novel Golding subtly shows the reader how he has shed all of his childhood names.

Using language to create a sense of place: setting

Golding sets the novel on an island, a place isolated from civilisation. This isolation means that the boys can have no contact with the outside world, so Golding can use this setting to explore how they begin to construct their own society. This microcosm of our world enables him to present the savagery and frailty of the human condition within this beautiful environment.

The island is presented as picturesque, with its beach and lush jungle. Golding uses precise geographical vocabulary to describe the features, for example, 'screes' to describe the rubble-like ground and 'half-cirque' economically describing a valley.

However, this island also holds darker elements. When we first see Ralph, a bird flashes upward with a sinister 'witch-like cry' and the 'creepers' catch and snag at Piggy as he tries to move. It is the boys though, who cause destruction within this paradise. The plane crash causes 'a scar' on the island. The first expedition sees Ralph, Jack and Simon heaving a rock off a cliff, foreshadowing the rock that kills Piggy, which symbolises the destruction of order and civilisation. The first fire kills the boy with the mulberry-coloured birthmark: the final fire causes the destruction of the fruit – their one constant food source. Through the boy's destruction of their environment, Golding is able to pinpoint the darkness at the heart of humankind. We see the boys within paradise destroying it because human nature cannot allow them to do anything else.

The Garden of Eden

The island can be seen to represent the Garden of Eden. In the Biblical story, Adam and Eve were placed in paradise by God. They were told not to eat from the Tree of Knowledge. The Devil, as a serpent, tempted Eve to eat the fruit and she in turn tempted Adam. When God saw their disobedience, he expelled them.

Ralph tells the boys that this is a 'good island'; it is only through their fear of the beast that the boys begin to think that the island might not be good. Notice how the boys get diarrhoea – mirroring the punishment for eating the 'forbidden fruit' in the Bible story. Adam and Eve's sin of eating the forbidden fruit is known as the 'original sin.'

(See page 82 for further Biblical allusion in the novel.)

DO IT!

The island is scarred by the boys. What scars might the boys have as a result of being on the island?

Structure

Plot structure

Freytag's pyramid

The 19th-century German novelist Gustav Freytag referred to plot structure as following five stages. This can be used to analyse the structure of *Lord of the Flies*. In this analysis we will see Ralph as the protagonist, 'the hero', and Jack as the antagonist, 'the villain.'

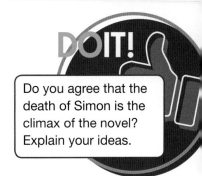

DO IT!

Do you agree that the death of Simon is the climax of the novel? Explain your ideas.

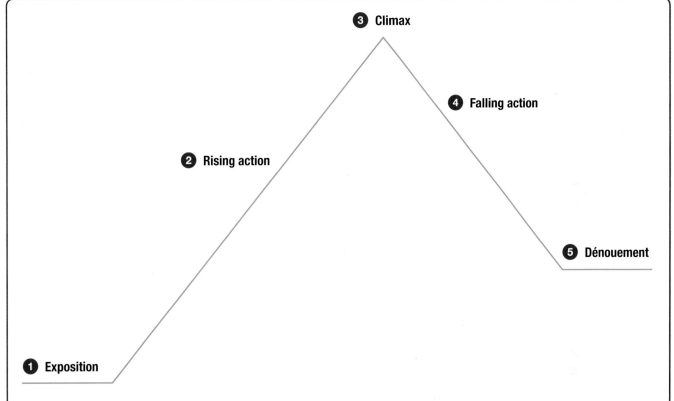

❸ Climax

❹ Falling action

❷ Rising action

❺ Dénouement

❶ Exposition

❶ Introduces the setting and the key characters. It also introduces the mood or atmosphere of the story.
The boys are on an island.
Jack and Ralph are established as key characters.
Ralph is elected as chief. This event moves the action to the next stage.

❷ Conflict is brewing. Obstacles stop the antagonist and the protagonist achieving their aims.
Tension begins to brew between Ralph and Jack. Obstacles appear: fear of the beast; failures to build shelters and to hunt successfully; hunters letting the fire go out when there's a passing ship; the dead parachutist – 'the beast' on the mountain. Finally, Jack's split from Ralph's group moves the action to the next stage.

❸ A turning point occurs where a change happens for better or worse for the protagonist.
The death of Simon occurs and with it the failure to hear Simon's message about the beast. Jack's power over the majority of the boys moves the action to the next stage.

❹ A reversal happens where the conflict between the protagonist and the antagonist begins to resolve. The protagonist can win or lose. Unexpected incidents increase the suspense.
Ralph is left with Piggy and Sam and Eric.
Suspense increases with the death of Piggy.
Ralph is alone. Suspense increases as Jack's tribe hunt Ralph and set fire to the island. Ralph's tumble on to the beach as the hunters close in prolongs the suspense.

❺ The end of the story. Characters can go back to normal lives – or a new normality. Catharsis – the final element of the ending – allows tension to dissolve.
Ralph looks up at the naval officer. Rescue has arrived. Catharsis: the 'trim cruiser' reminds the reader that the boys will return to another war – an adult war.

Structure of ideas

Golding's use of structure in the novel isn't only about plot structure. You can also look at how Golding structures his ideas.

Here, Golding develops the brutality of the deaths as the novel progresses. This shows the boys' descent into savagery as civilisation loses its influence on their behaviour.

Event	How Golding structures ideas
Death of the boy with the mulberry-coloured birthmark	Although the boys are not directly responsible for this death, it is their reckless actions that cause the fire to go out of control.
Death of Simon	It could be argued that the boys are caught up in the frenzy of the dance and the situation goes out of control. However, Golding presents Ralph's awareness of 'the thing we did' as an act that fills him with 'loathing' and a 'feverish excitement' at the same time.
Death of Piggy	The death of Piggy, caused by Roger levering a rock down on him, is seen as premeditated. It is Roger who, with 'delirious abandonment', leans on the lever – an action that is deliberate. Jack's reaction is to tell Ralph, 'That's what you'll get!'
Hunt for Ralph	The hunt for Ralph in the final chapter shows how far the boys' descent to savagery has taken them. There is a 'stick sharpened at both ends' presumably for Ralph's head. Luckily, the naval officer appears.

Golding uses this pattern again with throwing stones. Roger, at first, throws stones at Henry 'to miss'. This develops to throwing a stone 'between the twins…to miss.' At Castle Rock, he drops stones down on to Ralph and Piggy before sending down the final boulder that kills Piggy. We see clear steps progressing towards savagery.

Within the pig hunts, Jack's movement from the boy who couldn't kill the pig because of 'the enormity of the knife descending and cutting into living flesh' develops to the boy who 'twitched' as he tells Ralph, 'I cut the pig's throat', to the boy who leads a brutal and violent hunt on a sow who is feeding her young. This same boy will then begin a hunt for Ralph, someone for whom he once felt a 'shy liking'.

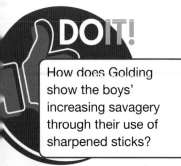

DO IT!

How does Golding show the boys' increasing savagery through their use of sharpened sticks?

Form

Allegory

The novel can be seen as an allegory. This is a story where the characters and events can be seen as symbols of wider events. In this way, the island can be seen as a microcosm of the world (literally meaning 'small world') and the boys can represent political perspectives, groups of people in society, or religious understanding.

Golding presents the boys as representing big ideas and concepts. **Ralph**, the protagonist, can be seen to represent democracy and civilisation, whereas **Jack**, the antagonist, can be seen to represent the opposing concepts of dictatorship and lust for power.

Piggy represents the voice of reason, intelligence and scientific thought. His glasses, symbolising clear-sightedness, are prized by the boys for their ability to create fire – a scientific innovation. Within society it is Ralph, representing civilisation, who values Piggy. The other boys ridicule him as he lacks the charisma that they see in Ralph's stillness and the thrill that Jack's hunting delivers. Society is seen to value charisma and excitement over intelligence and expert opinion.

Sam and Eric are the followers within this society. They are loyal to Ralph, yet are dominated by their fear of Jack's power and cruelty. This fear leads them to fall in with Jack's group. As the little people who speak with one voice, they cannot stand up to the autocratic leader.

The **littluns** represent the general public, whose daily lives are not touched by politics and struggles for power. They continue with their own world – their own bubble – playing and building sandcastles. Sadly, the general public will be drawn into the power games of an autocratic leader, reflecting what Golding saw during the Second World War in the lives of the ordinary people in Germany. By the end of the novel, the littluns are also painted, and part of the hunt for Ralph and Percival's inability to remember his address shows the reader how far he and the others have lost their grasp on civilisation.

Roger and **Simon**, like Ralph and Jack, represent opposite values within society. Simon represents goodness and spirituality whereas Roger can be seen as the representative of evil and brutality. We see Simon helping the littluns to reach inaccessible fruit to feed them, but we see Roger destroying their sandcastles, their games and throwing stones at them. Roger can be seen as the executioner and the torturer within the autocrat's rule. Interestingly, Simon arrived with Jack as a member of the choir, but more naturally works alongside Ralph to provide shelters (protection) for society.

(See page 82 for further discussion of Simon.)

STRETCHIT!

Within an allegory there is limited character development because the characters represent ideas. Do you think any of the characters in the novel develop as the novel progresses?

Symbols in the novel

Symbol	What it represents
the beast	The evil within all of us, which is why it is something we 'can't hunt or kill'; Simon recognises this, despite others trying to make the beast a physical being; it also represents fear and how fear can make us behave.
the conch 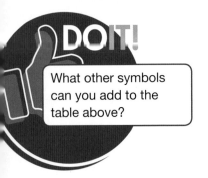	Order and the democratic right for everyone to have a voice: Piggy, as the voice of reason, values the conch; Jack does not. When Piggy dies, the conch is destroyed too: order and civilisation are lost from the island.
the fire	Rescue and protection, but it also represents destruction and the fires of hell.
painted faces	Savagery resulting in a loss of shame and self-consciousness, which can allow brutal and savage acts; it also acts as a mask to hide humanity.
the naval officer	Rescue on one level; however, his uniform and weapons of war symbolise the savagery that exists in war even when the uniform is clean and the cruiser 'trim'.

DO IT!

What other symbols can you add to the table above?

Some symbols in the novel can represent complex ideas with several layers of meaning, for example, adults. Parents within the adult world represent security, comfort and normality. However, the 'sign' from the adult world in the form of the dead airman brings fear and chaos to their society. The dead airman can also represent the turbulence warfare brings to the outside world.

Biblical allusion

As a character, Simon stands apart from the other boys and he can appear to be a puzzle when studying the novel. This is also true if you interpret the text as being a political allegory (see page 81). However, the novel's Biblical allusions help the reader to interpret his character.

Simon can be viewed as being a Christ-like figure within the novel. He is the only boy who does not give in to the temptations of savagery and remains good, untainted by evil, until his death.

Like Christ, Simon is seen helping others, especially the littluns. In the Bible, children were brought to Jesus to be blessed. The disciples, seeing the children as a nuisance, weren't happy, but the Bible shows Jesus replying, 'Let the little children come to me.' (Matthew 19: 13–14)

During his time in the sanctuary in the jungle, Simon talks with the Lord of the Flies. In the Bible, Jesus goes into the wilderness, where he is tempted by Satan yet avoids this temptation by quoting scriptures. Jesus also told his followers that 'the truth shall make you free' – that is, free from sin and death. When Simon returns from his sanctuary, with his truth, it is then that the boys murder him. Their descent into savagery – them giving into sin – means that Simon is unable to give them his truth. This truth, that it is a dead airman not the beast on the mountain and that the beast is within them all, is unable to set them free from their fear as Simon's message largely goes unheard.

The 'Lord of the Flies' refers to Beelzebub, in Christian sources another name for the Devil, or Satan. In the Testament of Solomon, a text associated with the Old Testament in the Bible, Beelzebub will cause jealousy and murders and bring on war. In the novel, when the boys give in to their savagery, linking them to the Devil, they set the island on fire, creating the fires of hell. In the Bible, it states that when the Devil rises the world will burn.

(For the novel's allusion to *The Coral Island* see page 16.)

REVIEW IT!

1 'Volleying shots' is a metaphor usually linked to what activity?

2 The 'swell' of the sea is like the 'breathing of some stupendous creature' is an example of what literary device?

3 Why does Golding set the novel on an island?

4 Give an example of Golding's use of foreshadowing in the novel.

5 What is a microcosm?

6 Give two examples of the boys' destruction of the island.

7 What Biblical story links to Golding's presentation of the island?

8 In Freytag's pyramid, what happens at the climax of any novel?

9 What is a protagonist and who is this on the island?

10 What is an antagonist and who is this on the island?

11 Name one **structural device** that Golding uses to show the development of the boys' savagery.

12 What is an allegory?

13 What does Piggy represent?

14 What does Roger represent?

15 What do the Littluns represent?

16 Explain the symbol of the fire in the novel.

17 What is allusion?

18 Name a novel that Golding alludes to in *Lord of the Flies*.

19 What other names are used for the 'Lord of the Flies'?

20 Explain how Simon can be viewed as a Christ-figure.

Doing well in your AQA exam

Understanding the question

Carefully preparing to answer the exam question is vital. If you are not clear in your mind about what the question is asking for, then there is a real risk that your answer will include irrelevant ideas and evidence.

Below is an AQA exam-style question. The question itself has been prepared by a student so that they fully understand it. Look at their notes.

NAILIT!

Read the question carefully and understand it. Make sure you focus on answering the question. Don't just write whatever you know about the novel. Your answer must be relevant to the question.

What methods and **techniques** does Golding use?

How does Golding make us feel about this issue?

What do the characters have to say about the role of civilisation?

What does Golding have to say about this theme?

AQA exam-style question

How does Golding present different attitudes to civilisation in *Lord of the Flies*?

Write about:

• what the different characters' attitudes are to the role of civilisation on the island

• how Golding presents attitudes to the role of civilisation by the way he writes.

Differences between society just after the Second World War and today

Differences between a reader just after the Second World War and today

This student has studied the question carefully and realised that:

• the focus is on the role of civilisation and characters' attitudes towards the role of civilisation

• 'presents' means how Golding creates and shapes the characters' speech and behaviour to explore this idea by identifying specific literary techniques

• 'civilisation' needs to be explored from two different viewpoints: the viewpoint of a reader just after the Second World War and the viewpoint of a modern reader

• what we think and feel about the characters' attitudes has been shaped and controlled by Golding.

'Pinning the question down' in this way has allowed the student to make sure that they have really thought about what the question is asking. In the exam room it is very easy to misread questions, answering the question that you want or expect to see, rather than the question that is actually there. The method outlined here will support you as you begin to find some useful ideas to support your answer.

DOIT!

Choose another question from earlier in this guide. 'Pin the question down' as above.

Planning your answer

You have 45 minutes for your response; 5–10 minutes spent preparing the question and planning your answer is time well used. It will help make sure your answer is clear and relevant. Practise preparing and planning.

Once you have pinned down your question properly, planning an answer will be quite straightforward. Your brief plan should set out:

- your key, *relevant* ideas
- the content of each of four or five paragraphs
- the order of the paragraphs.

Here is the same student's plan for the question on page 84. They have allowed 10 minutes for planning and 35 minutes for writing.

NAILIT!

High-level answers should have an overarching **argument** that is developed through the essay.

Paragraph	Content		Timing plan
1	Brief introduction. Use the words of the question and 'pinning the question down' to establish the focus of the answer and develop a line of argument.		9.15am
2	Ralph's understanding of civilisation: his focus on rescue and shelters; use of the conch and rules. What he represents.	Refer to reader reaction.	9.17am
3	Jack's opposing viewpoint: his focus on fun and thrill of the hunt; his flouting of rules and desire to punish and silence. What he represents.		9.24am
4	How the boys represent different groups in our civilisation. Microcosm of the real world. Who they follow. How and why this changes. Links to language, themes and contexts.		9.31am
5	Golding's message: that civilisation is held together by rules. There is evil within everyone. What happened in Germany 'It could happen here.'		9.38am
6	Brief conclusion. Refer back to question. Check answer.		9.45am

Sticking to the plan

Note how this student has jotted down time points for when they should move on to the next section of their answer. That way, they make sure they do not get stuck on one point and fail to cover the question focus in enough breadth.

Planning to meet the mark scheme

The plan above suggests that the student has thought carefully about the task in the question, that they are familiar with the mark scheme for their AQA Paper Two Modern Texts question and are planning to cover its requirements:

(See the mark scheme on pages 86–87.)

DOIT!

Go back to the exam question that you chose for the Do it on page 84. Develop a brief plan for it as above.

Assessment objective (AO)	What the plan promises
AO1 (Response to task and text)	Planning focuses on the question and the role of civilisation. Some personal responses to be included.
AO2 (Identification of writer's methods)	The presentation of Ralph and Jack's opposing views of civilisation and its importance. What Ralph and Jack as leaders represent – how Golding achieves this. Use of symbols. Use of language to show attitudes towards civilisation.
AO3 (Understanding of ideas/perspectives/context)	Links to the themes of civilisation, savagery and power. Links to Golding's message. Consideration of how the reader just after the Second World War and a modern reader would consider the role of civilisation in society.

What your AQA examiner is looking for

Your answer will be marked according to a mark scheme based on four assessment objectives (AOs). The AOs focus on specific knowledge, understanding and skills. AO4 – which is about vocabulary, sentence structures, spelling and punctuation – is worth just four marks. Together, the other AOs are worth 30 marks, so it is important to understand what the examiner is looking out for.

Mark scheme

Your AQA examiner will mark your answers in 'bands'. These bands loosely equate as follows:

- band 6 approx. grades 8 and 9
- band 5 approx. grades 6 and 7
- band 4 approx. grades 5 and 6
- band 3 approx. grades 3 and 4
- band 2 approx. grades 1 and 2.

Most importantly, the improvement descriptors in the table below will help you understand how to improve your answers and, therefore, gain more marks. The maximum number of marks for each AO is shown.

Assessment objective (AO)		Improvement descriptors				
		Band 2 Your answer…	**Band 3** Your answer…	**Band 4** Your answer…	**Band 5** Your answer…	**Band 6** Your answer…
AO1 12 marks	**Read, understand and respond**	is relevant and backs up ideas with references to the novel.	often explains the novel in relation to the question.	clearly explains the novel in relation to the question.	thoughtfully explains the novel in relation to the question.	critically explores the novel in relation to the question.
	Use evidence	makes some comments about these references.	refers to details in the novel to back up points.	carefully chooses close references to the novel to back up points.	thoughtfully builds appropriate references into points.	chooses precise details from the novel to clinch points.
AO2 12 marks	**Language, form and structure**	mentions some of Golding's methods.	comments on some of Golding's methods, and their effects.	clearly explains Golding's key methods, and their effects.	thoughtfully explores Golding's methods, and their effects.	analyses Golding's methods, and how these influence the reader.
	Subject terminology	sometimes refers to subject terminology.	uses some relevant terminology.	helpfully uses varied, relevant terminology.	makes thoughtful use of relevant terminology.	chooses subject terminology to make points precise and convincing.
AO3 6 marks	**Contexts**	makes some simple inferences about contexts.	infers Golding's point of view and the significance of contexts.	shows a clear appreciation of Golding's point of view and the significance of contexts.	explores Golding's point of view and the significance of relevant contexts.	makes perceptive and revealing links between the novel and relevant contexts.

AO1 Read, understand and respond/Use evidence

Make sure you read and answer the question carefully. Your examiner will be looking for evidence that you have answered the question given. Do not make the mistake of going into your exam with an answer in mind. Knowing the novel well will give you the confidence to show your understanding of the novel and its ideas as you answer the question on the paper in front of you.

Using evidence means supporting your ideas with references to the novel. They can be indirect references – brief mentions of an event or what a character says or does – or direct references – quotations. Choose and use evidence carefully so that it really does support a point you are making. Quotations should be as short as possible, and the very best ones are often neatly built into your writing.

AO2 Language, form and structure/Subject terminology

Remember that *Lord of the Flies* is not real life. It is a novel that Golding has *created* to entertain and influence the reader. The language and other methods he uses have been chosen carefully for effect. Good answers will not just point out good words Golding has used: they will explore the effects of those word choices on the reader. You must refer to the writer, showing that you understand that the novel is a construct at all times, to progress beyond Grade 3.

Subject terminology is about choosing your words carefully, using the right words and avoiding vague expressions. It is also about using terminology *helpfully*. For example, here are two different uses of subject terminology, the first much more useful than the second:

> ### Student answer A
>
> Golding uses the conch as a symbol of order and civilisation. Ralph uses it to impose order during assemblies through the rule that the boy holding the conch has the right to speak.

> ### Student answer B
>
> Golding uses the conch as a symbol. It is a pretty and delicate shell that makes a noise like a trumpet when blown.

AO3 Contexts

Context is important when it helps the reader to understand the meaning and ideas within the novel.

- How might the society Golding lived in have influenced his ideas and attitudes?

- How might the society *you* live in have influenced how you respond to ideas and attitudes in the novel?

- How might ideas and attitudes change over time for readers?

The best answers will include contextual information that is directly relevant to the *question*, not just the novel in general. (See pages 72–74 for more information and guidance on how to make the most of context in your writing.)

AO4: Vocabulary, sentence structures, spelling and punctuation

Make sure that you use a range of vocabulary and sentence structures for clarity, purpose and effect. Accurate spelling and punctuation is important too for this assessment objective.

NAILIT!

To boost your marks when answering questions do the following:

- Know the novel well. Read it and study it.

- Don't go into your exam with ready-prepared answers.

- Read the question and make sure you answer it thoughtfully.

- Choose details in the novel that will support your points.

- Don't treat the novel and its characters as though they are real. Instead, ask why Golding has chosen to create those words, or that event. What effect is he trying to achieve?

Writing your answer

Getting started

You have looked at one student's plan, and you will have noticed that they have decided to write a short introduction. Here are the openings of two students' answers to the question on page 84 about how Golding presents different attitudes to civilisation in *Lord of the Flies*.

Student answer A

Golding explores attitudes to civilisation through his presentation of the island as a microcosm of our society. Through this presentation, he explores opposing visions of civilisation through his characters, Ralph and Jack.

Student answer B

I am going to write about how Golding writes about civilisation. First I am going to talk about Ralph. Then I am going to talk about Jack. The novel was written in 1954 so civilisation was seen differently then. Those are the sorts of things I am going to write in my answer.

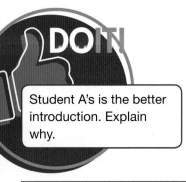

DOIT

Student A's is the better introduction. Explain why.

The response

Look at the student's plan for their essay on page 85. Here is part of the second paragraph of their answer. Note the way they use very brief quotations to help them comment on Golding's methods and their effects. An examiner has made some comments in the margin.

Golding presents Ralph's attitude towards civilisation as representing a democratic viewpoint. Ralph's first action as chief is to create a system for order during assemblies, as he tells the boys that they will 'have to have 'Hands up' like at school'. The reference to 'Hands up' and 'school' both imply that Ralph is seeking to recreate the order within civilisation that he knew before the island. Ralph follows this rule with a second rule that the 'conch' will be handed to the person, giving them the right to speak. Through this ruling, Ralph is establishing a democratic civilisation on the island where everyone has voice and a right to speak. Golding has already linked Ralph with the democratic process by him being voted into position as chief. The reader in 1954 and a modern reader would understand that laws and rules create order within our society and would recognise this attitude towards civilisation.

The words of the question are used to clearly focus on what is being asked.

Direct evidence used and neatly built into the student's own words.

Effect of the words is identified and analysed closely.

Using words from the question to keep on track

Confident focus on writer's craft.

Focus on context and reader reaction

Paragraph topics

The rest of your paragraphs should each deal with a subtopic of the main focus of the question. Here, the question focuses on Golding's presentation of the different attitudes towards civilisation. The student's plan suggests that the next three paragraph topics will be: Jack's opposing viewpoint to Ralph about civilisation, how the boys represent different groups in our civilisation and Golding's message.

The 'Golding's message' paragraph will help the student to address the 'How does Golding present' aspect of the question: in other words, the student can explore what Golding wanted the reader to learn and understand about attitudes towards civilisation.

Below you will see how – in part of their 'Jack' paragraph – the same student makes references to the themes in the novel in relation to the question. This shows that they understand that the novel is constructed to deliver Golding's viewpoint. The references are underlined to point them out.

> Jack, through his focus on hunting, shows a willingness to flout the rules as he <u>struggles to gain power over Ralph, a key theme in the novel</u>. He tells the boys that his leadership will provide fun and hunting something he sees as more important than a civilised society. Golding presents him angrily shouting, 'Bollocks to the rules!' showing that, <u>through savagery</u>, taboos about language are breaking down as well as <u>order and civilisation</u>. Jack's form of leadership shows that <u>his view of civilisation is gained through savagery and brutality</u>. His first thought about rule-breaking is that there should be 'punishments'. As Chief, Golding presents him ordering the beating of Wilfred for an unspecified crime - <u>the actions of an autocrat who is out of control with power</u>.

Using evidence:

This student uses **indirect evidence** by referring to the kind of words used when they are uncertain of the whole quotation and uses **direct evidence** in the form of quotations when they know them. Both forms of evidence are valid.

Ending your answer

If you write a conclusion, make it useful: don't simply repeat what you have already said. The answer we have been looking at ends with this summary:

> Golding presents his message that civilisation is held together by rules. Without these rules our society will descend into savagery that could lead to our society repeating the horrors that Golding saw during the Second World War.

DOIT!

Use the preparation and planning you did for your chosen exam question (see page 84) to write a full answer.

STRETCHIT!

Develop a range of evaluative vocabulary to enable you to pinpoint Golding's intention. Use words like:

- condemns
- criticises
- exposes
- ridicules
- subverts
- questions examines.

Going for the top grades

Of course you will always try to write the best answer possible, but if you are aiming for the top grades then it is vital to be clear about what examiners will be looking out for. The best answers will tend to:

• show a clear understanding of both the novel and the exam question • show insight into the novel and the question focus • explore the novel in relation to the focus of the question • choose evidence precisely and wisely	AO1
• analyse Golding's methods and their effect • use relevant, helpful subject terminology	AO2
• explore aspects of context that are relevant to the novel and question.	AO3

A great answer **will not** waste words or use evidence for its own sake.

A great answer **will** show that you are engaging directly and thoughtfully with the novel, not just scribbling down everything you have been told about it.

The best answers will be RIPE with ideas and engagement:

R	• Relevant	Stay strictly relevant to the question.
I	• Insightful	Develop relevant insights into the novel, its characters and themes.
P	• Precise	Choose and use evidence precisely so that it strengthens your points.
E	• Exploratory	Explore relevant aspects of the novel, looking at it from more than one angle.

Find an essay or practice answer you have written about *Lord of the Flies*.

Use the advice and examples on this page to help you decide how your writing could be improved.

Below is part of a student's answer to: How does Golding present different attitudes to civilisation? Next to the answer are some comments by an examiner.

What strikes me about Golding's presentation of attitudes towards civilisation is that, despite the naval officer appearing as rescue, therefore a force of good, he comes with all the trappings of warfare. His clean, white uniform is no different in intent from the savage's 'painted faces'. Its function is to show his belonging to a group, a naval force, and display his civilisation's power. Having served in the Navy during the Second World War, Golding was aware of the tensions between savagery that is condemned in society and the brutal acts that are sanctioned by society in warfare. It leaves the reader questioning how different the 'machine guns' and the revolvers are from the 'sticks sharpened at both ends'. The naval officer's attitude that the rules of civilisation would not be easily shaken off by 'British boys' is upset when Ralph answers his jovial question about 'Any dead bodies?' with the truth, 'only two.'

Clear and **nuanced** point.

Precise choice of evidence.

Original insight based on context

Precise evidence neatly integrated into argument

Good return to the question focus to maintain relevance

Golding's presentation of attitudes to civilisation explored here

REVIEW IT!

1 In your exam, how long should you spend preparing, planning and writing your *Lord of the Flies* answer?

2 Other than *Lord of the Flies*, what texts will you need to write about in Paper 2 (Modern texts)?

3 How many *Lord of the Flies* questions will there be on the paper?

4 How many questions should you answer on *Lord of the Flies*?

5 Here is a template for an essay question for *Lord of the Flies*. Create your own exam questions by filling in the brackets.
How and why does [name of character] change in *Lord of the Flies*? Write about:
- how [name of character] responds to other characters
- how Golding presents [name of character] in the way he writes.

6 Here is a template for an essay question for *Lord of the Flies*. Create your own exam questions by filling in the brackets.
How does Golding explore [theme] in *Lord of the Flies*? Write about:
- the ideas about [name of theme] in *Lord of the Flies*
- how Golding presents these ideas in the way he writes.

7 Here is a template for an essay question for *Lord of the Flies*. Create your own exam questions by filling in the brackets.
Do you think [name of character] is an important character in *Lord of the Flies*? Write about:
- how Golding presents [name of character]
- how Golding uses [name of character] to present ideas about [theme].

8 How long should you spend planning and preparing your answer?

9 Why is it important to prepare or 'pin down' your exam question?

10 What is meant by an indirect reference to the novel?

11 Why is it helpful to check your vocabulary, sentence structures, spelling and punctuation during your exam?

12 How many marks are AO1, AO2 and AO3 worth together?

13 What does AO1 test? How many marks are allocated out of 30?

14 What does AO2 test? How many marks are allocated out of 30?

15 Your friend has told you that they are going to learn an essay that they wrote in the mock exams as their revision. What would you say to them?

16 'Introductions and conclusions are not essential.' Is this true or false?

17 In the month leading up to your exam, what is a useful strategy to help you with your revision?

18 Plan a five-paragraph answer to the question you created in question 7 above. (Or you could use this question: Do you think Roger is an important character in *Lord of the Flies*? Write about:
- how Golding presents Roger
- how Golding uses Roger to present ideas about people and society.)

19 Plan a five-paragraph answer to the question you created for question 6 in this Review it quiz. (Or you could use this question: How does Golding explore friendships in *Lord of the Flies*? Write about:
- ideas about friendship in *Lord of the Flies*
- how Golding presents these friendships in the way he writes.)

20 Use the plan you made in question 18 or 19 above to write an answer in no more than 40 minutes.

NAILIT!

In the month leading up to your exam, all your revision should be based on planning and writing answers to exam questions. You will find plenty of exam questions in this guide for practice.

AQA exam-style questions

NAILIT!

Make sure that you only choose *one* question in your examination. The examiner will only give you marks for one response.

On these pages you will find six practice questions for *Lord of the Flies*. In your exam you will choose one question to answer from a choice of two. Quite often you will be presented with a question that focuses on character and a question that focuses on a theme or idea. Both questions carry the same marks.

PRACTICE QUESTION 1

How far does Golding present Simon as a spiritual character?

Write about:

- the way Simon is presented throughout the novel
- how Golding presents Simon by the way he writes about him.

[30 marks]
AO4 [4 marks]

PRACTICE QUESTION 2

How does Golding present different attitudes to hunting and killing?

Write about:

- what the different characters' attitudes are to hunting and killing
- how Golding presents attitudes towards hunting and killing by the way he writes.

[30 marks]
AO4 [4 marks]

PRACTICE QUESTION 3

How does Golding use Roger to explore ideas about evil?

Write about:

- how Golding presents the character of Roger
- how Golding uses Roger to explore ideas about evil.

[30 marks]
AO4 [4 marks]

PRACTICE QUESTION 4

How does Golding present Sam and Eric?

Write about:

- how Sam and Eric respond to Ralph and Jack

- how Golding presents Sam and Eric by the way he writes.

[30 marks]
AO4 [4 marks]

PRACTICE QUESTION 5

How does Golding use the littluns to explore ideas about the end of innocence?

Write about:

- how Golding presents the littluns

- how Golding uses these characters to explore ideas about the end of innocence.

[30 marks]
AO4 [4 marks]

PRACTICE QUESTION 6

How does Golding present human nature in *Lord of the Flies*?

Write about:

- how Golding presents aspects of human nature

- how Golding uses human nature to explore ideas about civilisation.

[30 marks]
AO4 [4 marks]

STRETCH**IT!**

Choose the question that you find most difficult. Use this guide and your notes to plan an answer to it.

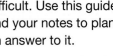

Glossary

allegory A story that can be interpreted to reveal a hidden meaning or message.

allusion Aiming to call to mind something that isn't mentioned directly (for example: Biblical stories or novels such as *The Coral Island*).

character A person in a play or story: a person created by the writer.

connotation The implied meaning of a word or phrase. For example, the word *mob* means a large group of people, but it *connotes* violence. If someone *dashes* down the road, we know that they are moving quickly, but that choice of word also connotes urgency. A connotation is sometimes called a **nuance**.

context The context of a poem, play, novel or story is the set of conditions in which it was written. These might include: the writer's life; society, habits and beliefs at the time they wrote; an event that influenced the writing; and the genre of the writing. The context is also seen in terms of influences on the reader; so, for example, a modern audience would see a Shakespeare play differently from audiences in his own time, as their life experiences would be different.

evidence Details or clues that support a point of view. A **quotation**, in which a few words are copied from a text to support a point of view, can be a form of evidence.

foreshadow A clue or a warning about a future event.

imagery The 'pictures' a writer puts into the reader's mind. **Similes** and **metaphors** are particular forms of imagery. We also talk about violent, graphic, religious imagery, and so on.

interpret To work out meaning, using clues and **evidence**. The same piece of writing can be interpreted in different ways, but evidence has to support interpretations.

language (choices) The words and the style that a writer chooses in order to have an effect on a reader.

metaphor Comparing two things by referring to them as though they are the same thing (for example: his face *was a thunder cloud*; the boy *was an angry bear*).

nuance Implied meaning: see **connotation**.

pathetic fallacy This is where nature (for example: weather) is used to reflect human emotions.

plot The plot of a literary text is the *story* – the narrative – or an interrelated series of events as described by the author.

quotation A word, phrase, sentence or passage copied from a text, usually used to support an argument or point of view. A quotation should be surrounded by inverted commas ('…'). It is usually wise to make quotations as short as possible, sometimes just one well-chosen word is enough.

setting The setting is the *time and place* in which a play or story takes place. The setting could also include the social and political circumstances (or **context**) of the action.

simile Comparing two things using either the word *like* or *as* (for example: the boy was *like an angry bear*; his running was *as loud as thunder*; her face was *as yellow as custard*).

slang Informal **language** (for example: *kid* rather than child; *grub* rather than food; *guys* rather than people).

structural device A feature used by a writer to give their writing shape and coherence. They include: **tone**; style; repetitions; extended images; shifts of focus, voice and **viewpoint**; openings and closings; sequencing of ideas; links between paragraphs and sentences.

subject terminology The technical words that are used for a particular subject. All the words in this glossary are subject terminology for English Literature.

technique Another word for method. Writers use different techniques to create different effects.

theme A theme is a central idea in a text. Common themes in novels, films, poems and other literary texts include: loyalty, love, race, betrayal, poverty, good versus evil, and so on.

tone The mood of a text, or the attitude of the author or narrator towards the topic. Tones can be mocking, affectionate, polite, authoritative, and so on.

viewpoint A writer's or **character's** point of view: their attitudes, beliefs and opinions.

vocabulary The words a writer chooses to use. They might use a particular sort of vocabulary (for example: formal, simple or shocking).

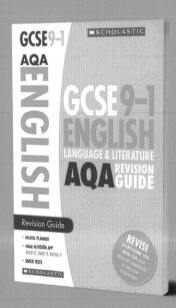